CELEBRATING THE MASS
THROUGHOUT THE YEAR

Celebrating the Mass Throughout the Year

Eucharist and the Liturgical Year

NATIONAL CENTRE FOR LITURGY

Published 2011 by
Veritas Publications
7–8 Lower Abbey Street
Dublin 1
Ireland
publications@veritas.ie
www.veritas.ie

ISBN 978 1 84730 273 1

10 9 8 7 6 5 4 3 2 1

A catalogue record for this book is available from the British Library.

Excerpts from the English translation of the *Roman Missal* © 2010, International Committee on English in the Liturgy, Inc. All rights reserved.

The English translation of *Universal Norms on the Liturgical Year and the Calendar* © 2010 International Committee on English in the Liturgy, Inc. All rights reserved.

Cover: Emmaus Supper by Ray Carroll. Used with permission.
This image was one of the treasures lost in the fire of Christmas morning 2009 in St Mel's Cathedral, Longford.

Designed by Colette Dower, Veritas Publications
Printed in the Republic of Ireland by Turners Printing Company Limited, Longford

CONTENTS

INTRODUCTION

Celebrating the Mass Throughout the Year was prepared by a team from the National Centre for Liturgy, including Moira Bergin, Jane Ferguson, Patrick Jones, Julie Kavanagh, Rosemary Lavelle, Columba McCann, Damian McNeice, Liam Tracey and Tom Whelan. It is offered as a study book for priests, on their own or in groups, for liturgy teams, for ministers of Word, music and Communion, for parishes, and for all who want to better understand the celebration of the Eucharist throughout the Liturgical Year.

Like *Celebrating the Mystery of Faith*, published by the National Centre for Liturgy as a study guide on the Mass, based on the *General Instruction of the Roman Missal*, some of the material uses pastoral notes prepared during the 1990s by ICEL. This material has been updated in the light of the new edition of the *Roman Missal* and its new translation.

There are many resources on the Liturgical Year and they remain as vital helps to all who prepare and celebrate our liturgy. The most important resources are the *Roman Missal*, the prayer book used at Mass, and the Lectionary, also part of the *Roman Missal* though published separately. To these must be added the *General Instruction of the Roman Missal* and the *Universal Norms on the Liturgical Year and Calendar*. The latter document is included here as an appendix.

Celebrating the Mass Throughout the Year underlines key elements for our celebration of the Eucharist through quoting the prayers of the *Roman Missal* and referencing the Scripture readings of the Lectionary. It is our hope that we may come to know many of these prayers and Scripture texts used at Mass in order to have a richer understanding of the celebration of the Paschal Mystery as it unfolds over the course of days, of weeks, and of the whole year (see Pope Paul VI's opening sentence in his Apostolic Letter approving the *Universal Norms for the Liturgical Year and Calendar*).

DOCUMENTS AND ABBREVIATIONS

Roman Missal   Third edition in new English translation, approved for use in the Dioceses of Ireland (2011)

Lectionary   Second edition (1981)

SC   Vatican II, The Constitution on the Sacred Liturgy, *Sacrosanctum concilium* (4 December 1963)

GIRM   *General Instruction of the Roman Missal*, including Adaptations for the Dioceses of Ireland (2005, in *Roman Missal* [2011])

LM   General Introduction, *Lectionary for Mass* (1981)

UNLYC   *Universal Norms for the Liturgical Year and the Calendar* (1969, in *Roman Missal* [2011])

PS   Congregation for Divine Worship, circular letter on the preparation and celebration of Easter, *Paschale solemnitatis* (1988)

DD   Pope John Paul II, Apostolic Letter, *Dies Domini*, On Keeping the Lord's Day Holy (1998)

RCIA   *Rite of Christian Initiation of Adults*, approved for the Dioceses of Ireland (1987)

MC   Pope Paul VI, Apostolic Exhortation, *Marialis Cultus*, for the right ordering and development of devotion to the Blessed Virgin Mary (1974)

CHAPTER ONE

THE LITURGICAL YEAR

Over the course of the year the Church celebrates the whole mystery of Christ, from the Incarnation to Pentecost Day and the days of waiting for the Advent of the Lord.[1]

☛   Take a copy of the *Roman Missal*, the book of prayers used at Mass, and examine the documents at the beginning. Some are documents giving approval to the Missal and approving it for use in the dioceses of Ireland. There is a lengthy document, ninety pages, entitled the *General Instruction of the Roman Missal (GIRM)*, the introduction to the Missal, both a 'how' and 'why' document in that it explains the way Mass is celebrated but also the understanding that lies behind it. Another but shorter document, nine pages, is the *Universal Norms on the Liturgical Year and the Calendar (UNLYC)*. It is followed by a series of tables, including the calendar for each month of the year.

    UNLYC gives an overview and understanding of the Liturgical Year, the annual cycle of feasts and seasons, with their traditional 'spiritual and bodily devotional practices, instruction, prayer, works of penance and works of mercy'.[2] Constant references are given to chapter V of the Constitution on the Sacred Liturgy, *Sacrosanctum concilium*, the first document given to the Church by the Second Vatican Council, formally promulgated on 4 December 1963. It remains a key document, being a charter for the renewal of the liturgical and prayer life of the Church. In the first four articles of chapter V, 102-104, in less than 370 words, there is a clear statement of what the Liturgical Year is and what makes the Liturgical Year.

☛   Read the following slowly. Highlight core phrases and words.

> *Church as Bride of christ*
>
> 102. Holy Mother Church is conscious that she must celebrate the saving work of her divine Spouse by devoutly recalling it on certain days throughout the course of the year. Every week, on the day which she has called the Lord's day, she keeps the memory of the Lord's resurrection, which she also celebrates once in the year, together with His blessed passion, in the most solemn festival of Easter.
>
> Within the cycle of a year, moreover, she unfolds the whole mystery of Christ, from the incarnation and birth until the ascension, the day of Pentecost, and the expectation of blessed hope and of the coming of the Lord. - *Eschatological - Parousia (2nd Coming - Greek for 'Presence')*
>
> Recalling thus the mysteries of redemption, the Church opens to the faithful the riches of her Lord's powers and merits, so that these are in some way made present for all time, and the faithful are enabled to lay hold upon them and become filled with saving grace.

---

[1] *UNLYC* 17.
[2] *UNLYC* 1.

103. In celebrating this annual cycle of Christ's mysteries, holy Church honours with especial love the Blessed Mary, Mother of God, who is joined by an inseparable bond to the saving work of her Son. In her the Church holds up and admires the most excellent fruit of the redemption, and joyfully contemplates, as in a faultless image, that which she herself desires and hopes wholly to be.

104. The Church has also included in the annual cycle days devoted to the memory of the martyrs and the other saints. Raised up to perfection by the manifold grace of God, and already in possession of eternal salvation, they sing God's perfect praise in heaven and offer prayers for us. By celebrating the passage of these saints from earth to heaven the Church proclaims the paschal mystery achieved in the saints who have suffered and been glorified with Christ; she proposes them to the faithful as examples drawing all to the Father through Christ, and through their merits she pleads for God's favours.

105. Finally, in the various seasons of the year and according to her traditional discipline, the Church completes the formation of the faithful by means of pious practices for soul and body, by instruction, prayer, and works of penance and of mercy.[3] *– E.g. fasting*

- In the liturgy of the Church we celebrate the saving work of the Risen Lord, the Paschal Mystery, his life and work, especially his death and resurrection, from the Incarnation to the Resurrection, the Ascension and the promise of the Holy Spirit.
- We gather in worship on certain days and at certain times and within the annual cycle; the mystery of Christ is unfolded, from his incarnation and birth – Christ's first coming – until Pentecost, waiting with hope for Christ's coming again in glory – his second coming among us.
- Keeping the memory of the Lord's resurrection, every week we celebrate the Lord's Day and every year the festival of Easter.
- Each year has its feasts and seasons, at times venerating Mary and the saints, at times keeping the traditional practice of preparing through fasting.

The times that mark the Liturgical Year are sketched out in the following chapters. But all these times have a unity because they are a celebration of the work of Christ, the Paschal Mystery. These times reach their most profound expression in the celebration of the Eucharist.

☞ Pray the following prayer:

Collect from the Votive Mass of the Most Holy Eucharist
O God, who have accomplished the work of human redemption
through the Paschal Mystery of your Only Begotten Son,
graciously grant that we, who confidently proclaim,
under sacramental signs, the Death and Resurrection of Christ,
may experience continued increase of your saving grace.
Through our Lord Jesus Christ, your Son,
who lives and reigns with you in the unity of the Holy Spirit,
one God, for ever and ever.
Amen.

---

[3] *SC* 102–105.

The following theological note comments on the above.

HOW WE UNDERSTAND TIME

The Human Experience of Time
We are accustomed, in society, to view 'time' as an entity that must be controlled, measured and used so as to bring about our secular salvation. We 'spend' time and 'waste' time. We create time and punctuate time, drawing on nature's cycles of day/night, seasons, tides …

Time grounds us in the present. Our sense of time gives us a relationship to the 'past' and a determination towards the 'future'. We expect that life's meaning will become clear 'in time', and 'time' is employed, in the absence of a faith context which would state otherwise, to *give meaning* to time.

A positive view of 'time' places importance on history and events as shaping how people think and live. Here 'time' has the possibility of enhancing the human experience while also contributing to an articulation of meaning that is expansive and open to the transcendent.

A Christian Understanding of Time
A Christian understanding situates 'time' between creation and the Parousia (the second coming of Christ). Then Christ will call 'all that does not resist love'[4] to its completion and fulfilment, so that God 'will be all in all' (1 Corinthians 15:28). For the Christian, time was elevated and made potentially salvific through the incarnation and birth of Jesus Christ, his first coming. God's definitive intervention in human history changed, not just the course of history, but an understanding of it. Thus, for the Christian, time has a particular meaning, context and purpose.

The Prologue to John's Gospel speaks of the eternal Word entering into our time, 'The Word was made flesh' (John 1:14). A period of 'preparation' is fulfilled by the coming of Christ ('Time of Christ') and extended, after the Ascension, in the 'Time of the Church'. Christ becomes the One who, coming from Eternity, initiates the 'last days'. He is the One who transforms the meaning of all time which urges us forward to the 'end-time', in eternity.

Jesus is the One who points to the fulfilment of time, who *is* in himself the fulfilment of history (see Galatians 4:4), and who gives meaning to everything that leads up to this completion.

The Christian understanding of time is not segmented, but is rather a continuum that stretches from the beginning to its point of completion in Christ. We are destined to find in this point of completion, which we will experience at the second coming, the culmination of our baptismal insertion into Christ (Romans 6:3-5).

The Christian Understanding of Time and the Realisation of the Kingdom
Considering time in its relationship to the Second Coming of Christ and its full implications brings in another vastly important consideration: time allows for the working out, through grace, of the kingdom transformation of the world and its values. This ultimate salvific purpose of God will be brought to completion and will not be frustrated. It is this end viewpoint that colours everything that Christians do and believe. Christian hope is never utopian but is, rather, deeply rooted in reality.

---

[4] A phrase from the theologian Karl Rahner.

TIME AND LITURGY

The Today of the Liturgy

Christian liturgy understands and employs time in a way different to that in which contemporary society does. Time is not simply something to be endured, to be filled, or to be enjoyed for its own sake. For the believer incorporated in Christ through baptism, time is a creative entity – salvifically creative – an ever present now which only has meaning in reference to the past (insofar as this past points us towards the future). But not just any past: a past which sees a continuum from the creation through the coming of Christ to his second coming.

In the liturgy we, in our 'present', summon the 'past' in view of our salvific future. This is brought together by the way we continually use the term 'Today' (*hodie*) in our prayer. The moments of Christ's life and ministry which were in the historical past become real for us 'today' (cf. Luke 4:21).

Inserted into the Mystery of Christ

In the very celebration of liturgy – every liturgy – we touch into the salvific reality of the Mystery of Christ. The entire life and ministry of Christ was salvific and was expressed in the most intense way in his saving passion, death, resurrection and ascension. We are invited, not simply to 'follow' Christ, but to continually allow ourselves to be more deeply inserted into the Mystery of Christ. Because liturgy operates sacramentally, it brings 'time' into the realm of 'eternity' and allows the eschatological, the 'end-time', become a reality for us now, even if we see and experience this imperfectly.

Chronos – Kairos

Liturgy allows the events of life to be considered in the context of salvation. Liturgy also allows the use of time, normally understood as the cyclic remembering of past events, to be treated in a *qualitative* way. The Greek word *chronos* can refer to time as a measured entity, whereas *kairos* speaks of the specific *quality* of an event in time as unexpected and coming from God's salvific bounty. To speak of *kairos* is to speak of time as charged with God's salvific presence, of time as being already imbued with eternity. Christ is this *kairos*, this 'fullness of time' (cf. Mark 1:15 and Galatians 4:4). Because liturgy actualises or makes real for us the decisive intervention of God in our history, then we must say that we celebrate liturgy in the realm of *kairos*.

Memory-Keeping in time

So much of liturgy operates cyclically. We have, for instance, a daily cycle of prayer, a weekly cycle initiated by the eighth day, monthly cycle of psalm readings, and an annual cycle of feasts, fasts and festivals. Related to all of this is the importance of 'memory' and time. The liturgy keeps memory of how God has worked 'for us and for our salvation' in the past, and how God continues to do that now in the present. In liturgy, this memory-keeping is effective, allowing those who gather in worship to participate in a real way in the 'event of Christ'. It is probably less about remembering the 'past' as making the salvific event, the Christ-event (of the historical past of Christ) present to us here and now. And this is in view of our future in Christ.

Purpose of the Liturgical Year

The liturgical year does not offer to us a series of pious ideas, nor does it attempt to simply celebrate the anniversaries of festivals relating to Christ. Rather it is an encounter with the saving God which is centered on the person of Christ in the Spirit. This is the Christ who revealed the saving will of a loving God in his incarnation, in his ministry of healing, through his miracles and teaching, his passion, saving death and life-giving resurrection, his ascension ... until he comes again in glory.

This Mystery of Christ continues to work 'for us and for our salvation' until 'he comes again in glory'. In a very real sense, we – in our time, our cultural context and place – are part of this final moment of salvation history, and it is through the liturgy that the Spirit of God actualises this for us.

All of this tells us that the purpose of the celebration of the liturgical year is a sacramental encounter that enables us, in a graced way, to be transformed into the likeness of Him who is love and who desires our salvation (1 Timothy 2:4) and thereby transform the world of which we are part into an anticipation, now, of the Kingdom. In our assembling, what we are doing is celebrating the entire saving mystery which is being placed before our eyes by the liturgy, an encounter with the living God.

☞ The celebration of the Mystery of Christ through the cycle of the liturgical year enables us to be transformed into the likeness of God and to, in turn, transform the world of which we are part. How does this statement influence our understanding and practice of the Eucharist and Mission?

Solemn Blessing for Easter (adapted)
May God, who by the Resurrection of his Only Begotten Son
was pleased to confer on us
the gift of redemption and of adoption,
give us gladness by his blessing.
R. Amen.

May he, by whose redeeming work
we have received the gift of everlasting freedom,
make us heirs to an eternal inheritance.
R. Amen.

And may we, who have already risen with Christ
in Baptism through faith,
by living in a right manner on this earth,
be united with him in the homeland of heaven.
R. Amen.

CHAPTER TWO

SUNDAY, THE DAY OF THE LORD

This is the day which the Lord has made: let us rejoice and be glad in it.
(Psalm 118:24)

The Church celebrates the Paschal Mystery – the suffering, death and resurrection of the Lord and the giving of the Spirit – on the first day of each week, known as the Lord's Day or Sunday. The fundamental importance of Sunday has been recognised through two thousand years of history and was emphatically restated by the Second Vatican Council:

> By a tradition handed down from the apostles which took its origin from the very day of Christ's resurrection, the Church celebrates the paschal mystery every eighth day; with good reason this, then, bears the name of the Lord's day or Sunday. For on this day Christ's faithful are bound to come together into one place so that, by hearing the word of God and taking part in the eucharist, they may call to mind the passion, the resurrection and the glorification of the Lord Jesus, and may thank God who 'has begotten them again, through the resurrection of Jesus Christ from the dead, unto a living hope' (1 Peter 1:3). Hence the Lord's day is the original feast day, and it should be proposed to the piety of the faithful and taught to them so that it may become in fact a day of joy and of freedom from work. Other celebrations, unless they be truly of greatest importance, shall not have precedence over the Sunday which is the foundation and kernel of the whole liturgical year.[1]

While the Paschal or Easter Triduum is the great annual Christian celebration, Sunday is the weekly remembrance of the Easter mystery.

SUNDAY, THE LORD'S DAY

In Latin, Sunday is *Dominica* or *Dominica dies*, the day on which the risen Christ manifested himself as Lord. The Irish word for Sunday takes two forms: 'An Domhnach' and 'Dia Domhnaigh'; both signify 'the Day of the Lord'. The Church has referred to Sunday as 'The Lord's Day' because at its very core is the Christian mystery. This is a tradition going back to the Apostles, taking its origin from the actual day of Christ's Resurrection.

Sunday is the Easter which returns week by week, celebrating Christ's victory over sin and death, the fulfilment in him of the first creation and the dawn of 'the new creation' (cf. 2 Corinthians 5:17). The Resurrection of Jesus is the fundamental event upon which Christian faith rests (cf. 1 Corinthians 15:14). Throughout the gospel accounts, there is a reference to the first day of the week as the day of the Lord's rising from the dead and the Church first believing in his Resurrection. It is also on this first day that the disciples at Emmaus recognise the Lord in the breaking of the bread (Luke 24:13-35). The First Day of the Week refers to the story of creation; God began the work of creation on the 'first day of the week'. But Christians also refer to this day which follows the Sabbath as 'the Eighth Day'. This symbolically confirms that because of the resurrection of Christ something new was happening.

---

[1] *SC* 106.

SUNDAY AND EUCHARIST

The first Christians received from Judaism a rich heritage of patterned time, of feasts and fasts. The only new Christian feast that we know to have existed in New Testament times was the weekly feast of Sunday. It is 'the original feast'. Sunday was the day when Christians gathered in memory of Christ. This Sunday gathering gave them their identity. Writing around the year 150, Saint Justin uses the language of the time to note that Christians gather together 'on the day named after the sun' but for believers the expression had already assumed a new meaning which was unmistakably rooted in the Gospel. He wrote that Christians gathered because it was 'the first day', recalling creation, but also 'the day on which Jesus Christ our Saviour rose from the dead'.

In our own time, Pope John Paul II, now beatified, wrote an Apostolic Letter in 1988 on Sunday, called *Dies Domini*. He saw Sunday as the day of faith, writing:

> Yes, Sunday is the day of faith. This is stressed by the fact that the Sunday Eucharistic liturgy, like the liturgy of other solemnities, includes the Profession of Faith. Recited or sung, the Creed declares the baptismal and Paschal character of Sunday, making it the day on which in a special way the baptised renew their adherence to Christ and his Gospel in a rekindled awareness of their baptismal promises. Listening to the word and receiving the Body of the Lord, the baptised contemplate the Risen Jesus present in the 'holy signs' and confess with the Apostle Thomas: 'My Lord and my God!' (John 20:28).[2]

The Apostolic Letter stresses that Sunday is an indispensable element of our Christian identity. It is not only the remembrance of a past event: it is a celebration of the living presence of the Risen Lord in the midst of his own people. God's people gathered embodies from age to age the image of the first Christian community. St Luke, writing in the Acts of the Apostles, presents a picture of the lifestyle of the first baptised believers who 'devoted themselves to the apostles' teaching and fellowship, to the breaking of bread and the prayers' (Acts 2:42). This ecclesial dimension intrinsic to the Eucharist is realised in every Eucharistic celebration and is expressed particularly on the day when the whole community comes together to commemorate the Lord's Resurrection. The *Catechism of the Catholic Church* is referred to where it teaches that 'the Sunday celebration of the Lord's Day and his Eucharist is at the heart of the Church's life'.[3] The disciples at Emmaus recognising the Risen Lord in the breaking of bread has already been mentioned. Again, the connection between the presence of the Risen Lord and Eucharist is noted. They recognised him when he 'took the bread, said the blessing, broke it and gave it to them' (Luke 24:30). The gestures of Jesus in this account are the same as at the Last Supper. The 'breaking of bread' was the name given to the Eucharist by the first generation of Christians.

WHAT SUNDAY IS

Blessed John Paul II uses five titles for Sunday, to each of which a chapter is given. He wrote, 'The duty to keep Sunday holy, especially by sharing in the Eucharist and by relaxing in a spirit of Christian joy and fraternity, is easily understood if we consider the many different aspects of this day upon which the present Letter will focus our attention.'[4]

Dies Domini (**The Day of the Lord**): Though Sunday is the festival of the 'new creation', it is also the celebration of the work of God the creator. 'This aspect is inseparable from what the first pages of Scripture tell us of the plan of God in the creation of the world.'[5]

---

[2] *DD* 29.
[3] *CCC* 2177.
[4] *DD* 7.
[5] *DD* 8.

Dies Christi (**The Day of Christ**): Sunday is the weekly Easter, the day of the Risen Lord. As well as being 'the day of light', Sunday is also 'the day of 'fire', referring to the outpouring of the Spirit, the great gift of the Risen Lord to his disciples on Easter Sunday.[6]

Dies Ecclesiae (**The Day of the Church**): At the heart of Sunday is the gathering of God's people to celebrate the Eucharist. In the words of the *Didascalia Apostolorum*, a third century text written in Syria: 'Leave everything on the Lord's Day and run diligently to your assembly, because it is your praise of God. Otherwise, what excuse will they make to God, those who do not come together on the Lord's Day to hear the word of life and feed on the divine nourishment which lasts forever?'[7]

Dies Hominis (**The Day of Humankind**): The Christian Sunday fulfils the Old Testament Sabbath and is a day of joy, rest and solidarity. 'To experience the joy of the Risen Lord deep within is to share fully the love which pulses in his heart: there is no joy without love!'[8]

Dies Dierum (**The Day of Days**): At Easter we acclaim the Risen Christ as 'the Beginning and End, the Alpha and Omega'. As the weekly Easter, Sunday also reveals the meaning of time; it 'foreshadows the last day, the day of the *Parousia*, which in a way is already anticipated by Christ's glory in the event of the Resurrection.'[9]

St Justin, a convert to Christianity, wrote a defense of the Christian faith and practice, addressed to the Emperor Antoninus Pius and his son Marcus Aurelius in the *First Apology*, around the year 150. He described the Eucharist celebrated following a Baptism:

> After the prayers, we greet one another with a kiss.
>
> Then bread and a cup of wine mixed with water are brought to the one presiding, who gives praise and glory to the Father of the universe, through the name of the Son and of the Holy Spirit and offers thanksgiving at length because the Father has counted us worthy to receive these gifts. When the prayer of thanksgiving is ended, all the people present give their assent with an 'Amen'. ('Amen' in Hebrew means 'So be it'.) …

Justin offered a second account in which he described the Sunday Eucharist:

> And on the day named after the Sun, all who live in cities and countryside assemble in one place, and the memoirs of the apostles or the writings of the prophets are read for as long as time permits.
>
> When the reader has finished, the one presiding addresses us, instructing us and exhorting us to imitate the splendid things we have heard.
>
> Then we all stand and pray and when we have finished praying, bread, wine and water are brought forward. The one presiding offers the prayer of thanksgiving, according to his ability, and the people assent, saying 'Amen'. Then the gifts over which the thanksgiving has been spoken are distributed and each one share in them, while the deacons bring them to those who are absent.

---

[6] *DD* 28.
[7] Cf. *DD* 46.
[8] *DD* 69.
[9] *DD* 75.

A collection is taken from those who can afford to contribute, each as they please, and it is given to the one who has presided to help orphans and widows, who are in need through sickness or some other reason, those in prison, and visiting strangers; in a word, the one presiding takes care of all in need.

The reason why we call assembly on the day named after the Sun is that it is the first day, the day on which God transformed darkness and matter and created the world, and the day on which Jesus Christ our Saviour rose from the dead.

☛ Retell or rewrite Justin's description of the Sunday Eucharist using today's terminology; for example, 'Sunday' for 'the day named after the Sun', 'the Eucharistic Prayer' for 'the prayer of thanksgiving'.

SUNDAY EUCHARIST: GIVING THANKS

The Eucharistic Prayer is 'the centre and high point of the entire celebration' and is a 'prayer of thanksgiving and sanctification'.[10] Thanksgiving is one of its main elements. 'The thanksgiving (expressed especially in the Preface), in which the priest, in the name of the whole of the holy people, glorifies God the Father and gives thanks to him for the whole work of salvation or for some particular aspect of it, according to the varying day, festivity, or time of year.'[11]

Let us give thanks to the Lord our God
It is right and just.
It is truly right and just, our duty and our salvation
always and everywhere to give [God] thanks …

Then follows a powerful expression of thanksgiving before, joining with the angels and saints, we acclaim:

Holy, Holy, Holy Lord God of hosts.
Heaven and earth are full of your glory.
Hosanna in the highest.
Blessed is he who comes in the name of the Lord.
Hosanna in the highest.

The Missal has eight prefaces for Sundays in Ordinary Time. Under eight themes, they express our thanksgiving on Sundays as we pray to God in the name of Christ our Lord:

I. *The Paschal Mystery and the People of God*
For through his Paschal Mystery,
he accomplished the marvellous deed,
by which he has freed us from the yoke of sin and death,
summoning us to the glory of being now called
a chosen race, a royal priesthood,
a holy nation, a people for your own possession,
to proclaim everywhere your mighty works,
for you have called us out of darkness
into your own wonderful light.

---

[10] *GIRM* 78.
[11] *GIRM* 79.

II. *The mystery of salvation*
For out of compassion for the waywardness that is ours,
he humbled himself and was born of the Virgin;
by the passion of the Cross he freed us from unending death,
and by rising from the dead he gave us life eternal.

III. *The salvation of man by a man*
For we know it belongs to your boundless glory,
that you came to the aid of mortal beings with your divinity
and even fashioned for us a remedy out of mortality itself,
that the cause of our downfall
might become the means of our salvation,
through Christ our Lord.

IV. *The history of salvation*
For by his birth he brought renewal
to humanity's fallen state,
and by his suffering, cancelled out our sins;
by his rising from the dead,
he has opened the way to eternal life,
and by ascending to you, O Father,
he has unlocked the gates of heaven.

V. *Creation*
For you laid the foundations of the world
and have arranged the changing of times and seasons;
you formed man in your own image
and set humanity over the whole world in all its wonder,
to rule in your name over all you have made
and for ever praise you in your mighty works,
through Christ our Lord.

VI. *The pledge of the eternal Passover*
For in you we live and move and have our being,
and while in this body
we not only experience the daily effects of your care,
but even now possess the pledge of life eternal.
For, having received the first fruits of the Spirit,
through whom you raised up Jesus from the dead,
we hope for an everlasting share in the Paschal Mystery.

VII. *Salvation through the obedience of Christ*
For you so loved the world
that in your mercy you sent us the Redeemer,
to live like us in all things but sin,
so that you might love in us what you loved in your Son,
by whose obedience we have been restored to those gifts of yours
that, by sinning, we had lost in disobedience.

VIII. *The Church united by the unity of the Trinity*
For when your children were scattered afar by sin,
through the Blood of your Son and the power of the Spirit,
you gathered them again to yourself,
that a people, formed as one by the unity of the Trinity,
made the body of Christ and the temple of the Holy Spirit,
might, to the praise of your manifold wisdom,
be manifest as the Church.

☛ Read the above excerpts from the Sunday Prefaces. Note that 'you' refers to God to whom we are praying but 'he' and 'his' in I, II and IV refer to Christ.

☛ Why are we offering God thanks on this day, on this Sunday?

☛ What did Christ do among us and for us?

We cannot live without Sunday
Sine dominico non possumus

In the year 304, forty-nine Christians from Abitina (or Abitene), a city of the Roman province, near Carthage in north Africa, were martyred. Under the persecution of the Emperor Diocletian, Christians were forbidden to gather for worship. Disobeying the Emperor, they gathered each week to celebrate Mass on Sundays. At a gathering in the house of Ottavio Felice, they were arrested. On trial in Carthage, Proconsul Anulinus said to Felice, 'I am not asking you if you are a Christian, but if you have taken part in the assembly.' The account of the trial comments that this is a foolish and ridiculous question, as to be without the Sunday Eucharist is an impossibility for a Christian. It is the Sunday Eucharist which makes the Christian. Emeritus, a reader, was questioned, 'Why have you received Christians in your home, transgressing the orders of the Emperor?' He answered, *'Sine dominico non possumus'* (We cannot live without Sunday). Without Sunday and without Sunday Mass, we cannot live.

☛ Sunday Mass is a vital factor for our identity as Christian. Discuss the consequences of the situation where many don't attend Mass or do so very irregularly or only on special occasions.

SUNDAY THROUGHOUT THE LITURGICAL YEAR

Ordinary Time begins on the Monday after the Sunday following 6 January, the solemnity of the Epiphany, and continues until the Tuesday before Ash Wednesday inclusive. It begins again on the Monday after Pentecost and ends before Evening Prayer I of the First Sunday of Advent. Ordinary Time comprises thirty-three or thirty-four weeks.

The numbering of Sundays in Ordinary Time is computed in this way: the first week in Ordinary Time follows the feast of the Baptism of the Lord. The other Sundays and weeks are numbered in order until the beginning of Lent. If there are thirty-four weeks in Ordinary Time, the numbering of the weeks resumes after Pentecost, even though the solemnities of the Most Holy Trinity and of the Most Holy Body and Blood of Christ (Corpus Christi) are celebrated in many countries, including Ireland, on the first two Sundays after Pentecost. If there are thirty-three weeks in

Ordinary Time, the first week that would otherwise follow Pentecost is omitted. The thirty-fourth Sunday, at the beginning of the last week of Ordinary Time before Advent, is the solemnity of Our Lord Jesus Christ, Universal King.

The transitions between seasons deserve attention in order to enhance the rhythm of the Liturgical Year. After the feasts of the Epiphany and the Baptism of the Lord, the Sunday gospels concentrate on the beginnings of the Lord's preaching. As the Year draws to a close and Advent approaches, eschatological themes, that is, about the end of time or the Coming of the Lord in glory, predominate.

While the season of Easter and Lent, Advent and Christmas have their own distinctive character and celebrate a specific aspect of the mystery of Christ, the weeks in Ordinary Time, especially the Sundays, are devoted rather to the mystery of Christ in all its aspects.[12]

THE INTEGRITY OF THE SUNDAY CELEBRATION

The integrity of the Sunday should always be respected. Only the most solemn feasts, like the Most Holy Trinity, the Most Holy Body and Blood of Christ, All the Saints, the Assumption of the Blessed Virgin Mary, when they occur on a Sunday, take precedence. While on occasion it may be appropriate to celebrate a Ritual or special Mass on a Sunday in Ordinary Time, this should only occur when a serious need or pastoral advantage is present and at the direction of the local Ordinary or with his permission.

Where there are themes proposed for Sundays, for example, Christian unity, vocations, Christian education, they do not change the liturgical calendar or displace the regular Sunday liturgy. They may be referred to in the homily when appropriate to the prayers and readings of the day's liturgy. They may be expressed in the Universal Prayer or Prayer of the Faithful, mentioned at the time of the announcements, and reflected in the decoration of the church.

Further treatment of Sunday is given later in the chapters on Ordinary Time and the seasons.

☞ Given what you have explored about Sunday and its importance, discuss the ways in which the parish celebration of Mass on a Sunday should differ to the celebration of Mass during the week.

---

[12] *UNLYC* 43.

CHAPTER THREE

ORDINARY TIME

Celebrating the mystery of Christ in all its aspects [1]

The entire year is an unfolding in the liturgy of the Mystery of Christ. [2] 'Ordinary Time', while being less intense than the festivals around the Incarnation (Christmas Season) or the death and resurrection of Christ (Easter Season), opens up to us the same saving event of Christ so that our sense of 'time' is transformed as well as sanctified. The weeks of Ordinary Time, especially the Sundays, are devoted to the mystery of Christ in all its aspects. [3]

> *Common Preface V: The Proclamation of the Mystery of Christ*
> It is truly right and just, our duty and our salvation,
> always and everywhere to give you thanks,
> Lord, holy Father, almighty and eternal God,
> through Christ our Lord.
>
> His Death we celebrate in love,
> his Resurrection we confess with living faith,
> and his Coming in glory we await with unwavering hope.
>
> And so, with all the Angels and Saints,
> we praise you, as without end we acclaim:
>
> Holy, Holy, Holy Lord God of hosts …

GOD'S TIME AND OUR TIME

The liturgical seasons of the year help us to focus on central aspects of the one saving Mystery of Christ. Through their yearly cycle, we allow these seasons to colour the way we pray and sing, what readings we proclaim, and how all of this shapes our Christian living.

'Ordinary Time' relates intimately with the liturgical seasons. From the more intense concentration on the Incarnation of Christ (Christmas) and his death and resurrection (Easter), the prayers and readings of Ordinary Time offer us an opportunity to focus in on the mediation of God in the daily events of our lives and history.

While this dynamic happens at all times, Ordinary Time allows us to give particular expression to the intersection between God's time (*kairos*) and our time (*chronos*). We are used to celebrating events in our lives in annual or yearly cycles. For the Christian the entire liturgical year, but especially Ordinary Time, allows us to interpret *our* time (*chronos*) in the context of *God's* time (*kairos*).

---

[1] See *UNLYC* 43.
[2] *SC* 102.
[3] *UNLYC* 43.

The extraordinary salvific giftedness of God allows us to 'read' our daily lives in a different way, offering to us an opportunity to give sacramental character to the way in which we use 'time'.

COUNTED – ORDINAL TIME

The term 'ordinary' should not be interpreted as meaning that this time in the liturgical year is mundane or trivial. Rather the term 'ordinary' comes from the word for ordinal or counted time. The Sundays in Ordinary Time are thus signified by number, for example the Fifth Sunday, the Twenty-First Sunday or the Thirty-Third Sunday in Ordinary Time. On the Sundays of Ordinary Time we continue to celebrate the extraordinary events of life, death, resurrection and ascension of Christ.

ORDINARY TIME AND LITURGY: PASTORAL CONSIDERATIONS

The integrity of the yearly liturgical cycle

While special themes or 'Days of Prayers' are proposed for Sundays, they do not, with the exception of Mission Sunday, displace the regular Sunday liturgy, thus ensuring an integrity for the Lord's Day and its celebration of Eucharist.

We need to maintain a balance between how we relate the liturgical year with the civil year. On the one hand, we need to bring our celebration of the civil year to bear on how we celebrate the Mystery of Christ in its various expressions throughout the year. We do this so as to help us transform our history through God's action in us and make it more reflective of the Kingdom. Yet, in order to retain its integrity, we need to ensure that the liturgical unfolding of the event of Christ in an annual cycle is conceived as a unity and not primarily or simply as something to be aligned with the civil year.

A time to establish good patterns of worship

Good quality in liturgical celebration should be maintained throughout Ordinary Time, as in all the seasons of the Liturgical Year. Ordinary Time offers an opportunity for communities to reflect on their liturgical practice and make any necessary changes for the enhancement of the celebration of liturgy. It is a time to look back to basics and evaluate local practice.

The planning and preparation of the liturgy should seek to develop consistent patterns for both ministers and the assembly as they fulfil their respective roles in the celebration of the Eucharist. Such patterns can be achieved without the loss of appropriate variety in the choice of texts and ritual elements for particular celebrations.

By paying attention to and providing for the good celebration of liturgy, liturgical ministers will be well prepared for their tasks, and the actions and objects used will have the strength and clarity of symbols that are effective.

The colour and décor of Ordinary Time

Vestments are green in colour for Sundays and weekdays. Decorations may appropriately reflect the beauty of nature and the changes in the local natural environment.

☞ Use the companion book, *Celebrating the Mystery of Faith: A Guide to the Mass*, for further considerations on the preparation and celebration of Mass.

THE LECTIONARY IN ORDINARY TIME

Weekday Readings

In the readings for Mass, we have unfolded before us the life and teaching of Christ.[4] The weekdays in Ordinary Time provide, in a semi-continuous series, gospel readings from the synoptic gospels, that is, Matthew, Mark and Luke. This cycle is repeated every year, and we are often offered a more complete reading of the individual gospels, with the inclusion of some passages omitted in the Sunday cycle of readings.

Weekday Gospel Readings in Ordinary Time
Weeks 1–9 Mark
Weeks 10–21 Matthew
Weeks 22–34 Luke

Readings from the Old Testament and from one or other of the Apostles, in a semi-continuous series, occur in a two-year cycle.

Weekday liturgies will be varied with the keeping of the memory of a saint or, when appropriate, a Mass for Various Needs and Occasions with the appropriate prayers. Occasionally one or both readings are integral to the celebration of a memorial of a saint or to bring out some particular aspect of a saint's life. However, the Lectionary offers readings for all saints, but on these occasions the integrity of the weekday lectionary should be respected to the extent possible, and these weekday readings should be replaced only when, in the judgement of those responsible for the preparation of the liturgy, it would be pastorally beneficial to use other readings from the Lectionary.[5]

Common Preface IV: Praise, the Gift of God
It is truly right and just, our duty and our salvation,
always and everywhere to give you thanks,
Lord, holy Father, almighty and eternal God.

For, although you have no need of our praise,
yet our thanksgiving is itself your gift,
since our praises add nothing to your greatness
but profit us for salvation,
through Christ our Lord.

And so, in company with the choirs of Angels,
we praise you, and with joy we proclaim:

Holy, Holy, Holy Lord God of hosts …

Sundays in Ordinary Time

The Sundays of Ordinary Time follow the three-year lectionary pattern, providing a semi-continuous reading of the Gospels of Matthew, Mark and Luke over a three-year cycle on the Sundays in Ordinary Time in such a way that, as the Lord's life and preaching unfold, the teaching proper to each of these gospels is presented.

For this reason, the integrity of the Lectionary is respected, and the homily at the Sunday Eucharist normally draws upon the Scriptures to open up for the assembly the mysteries of the faith and the

---

[4] *LM* 105.
[5] See *LM* 83.

guiding principles of the Christian life. In this way, the celebration of the mystery of Christ is connected with the everyday life and commitments of the Christian people who make up the assembly.

Thanks to the continuity of the scriptural texts used on Sundays, the liturgy sometimes commemorates a certain aspect of Christ's life and ministry over a period of several weeks, for example, the Sermon on the Mount from the Fourth Sunday to the Ninth Sunday in Year A and the five weeks in Year B when the reading of chapter six of the Gospel of John is inserted into the cycle of Mark's Gospel. It can be helpful in planning the Sunday liturgy to take notice of these elements of unity.

Lectionary Year A – Year of Matthew*

In order to do justice to the intention of the Lectionary, the five great 'sermons' in Matthew's Gospel will of necessity be the focal points of preaching and instruction. The narrative sections, which are placed between the sermons, are composed in such a way that there is a unity and coherence in the whole work. Discourse and narrative stand side by side, so that the narrative chapters prepare the way for what follows in the discourses. Recognising the way in which the Lectionary has reflected the structure of Matthew's Gospel will enable preachers and readers to see the context of the readings from one week to the next.

Unit I	The figure of Jesus the Messiah	
	The baptism of Jesus; the witness of John the Baptist	Sundays 1–2
Unit II	Christ's design for life in God's kingdom	
	Narrative: the call of the first disciples	
	Discourse: the sermon on the mount	Sundays 3–9
Unit III	The spread of God's kingdom	
	Narrative: the call of Levi	
	Discourse: the mission sermon	Sundays 10–13
Unit IV	The mystery of God's kingdom	
	Narrative: the revelation to the simple	
	Discourse: the parable sermon	Sundays 14–17
Unit V	God's kingdom on earth – the Church of Christ	
	Narrative: the feeding of five thousand; Jesus walks on the waters;	
	the Canaanite woman; Peter's confession – the primacy conferred;	
	the passion prophesied – discipleship	
	Discourse: the community sermon	Sundays 18–24
Unit VI	Authority and invitation – the ministry ends	
	Narrative: the parables of the labourers, the two sons,	
	the wicked vinedressers, and the marriage feast	
	Discourse: the final sermon	Sundays 25–33
Unit VII	God's kingdom fulfilled	
	Christ the King	Sunday 34

---

* These charts are based on the writings and lectures of the late John H. Fitzsimmons. See *LM* footnote 102, introduction to second edition and tables.

Lectionary Year B – Year of Mark

Mark's main interest is the person of Jesus himself. He follows Jesus through his public ministry in Galilee, outside Galilee and finally in Jerusalem itself immediately before the Passion. The crisis is reached when the fundamental question is posed to the disciples: 'Who do you say I am?' Peter's confession of faith is, therefore, at the heart of Mark's Gospel. In the Year of Mark the Lectionary observes faithfully the structure and message of the Gospel itself. One important peculiarity is that the Lectionary includes a major insert from the Gospel of John (Sundays 17–21: John 6 – the sermon on the 'Bread of Life'). This fits into this part of Mark's Gospel, which is concerned with Jesus' revelation of himself, and is known as 'the Bread section'.

Unit I	The figure of Jesus the Messiah	Sundays 1–2
Unit II	The mystery progressively revealed	Sundays 3–23
	Stage 1 Jesus with the Jewish crowds	Sundays 3–9
	Stage 2 Jesus with the disciples	Sundays 10–14
	Stage 3 Jesus manifests himself	Sundays 15–23
Unit III	The mystery of the Son of Man	Sundays 24–34
	Stage 1 The 'Way' of the Son of Man	Sundays 24–30
	Stage 2 Final revelation in Jerusalem	Sundays 31–33
	Stage 3 The fulfilment of the mystery	Sunday 34

Lectionary Year C – Year of Luke

Luke's Gospel represents Jesus' journey from Galilee to Jerusalem – a journey which is completed in the Acts of the Apostles by the journey of the Church from Jerusalem 'to the end of the earth'. The Lectionary in the Year of Luke represents faithfully his 'Travel Narrative' (chapters 9–19) – Jesus' journey to death, to resurrection and his return to the Father (see Sundays 13–31). Luke's vision of the journey is not geographical or chronological. Rather, it is seen as a journey for the whole Church and for the individual Christian, a journey towards suffering and glory. Each Gospel passage should mean a great deal more to a preacher and reader when it is seen in the context of the whole programme of readings for Year C.

Unit I	The figure of Jesus the Messiah	Sundays 1–2
Unit II	Luke's programme for Jesus' ministry	Sundays 3–4
Unit III	The Galilean Ministry	Sundays 5–12
Unit IV	The first part of the 'Travel Narrative': the qualities Jesus demands of those who follow him	Sundays 13–23
Unit V	The 'Gospel within the Gospel': the message of pardon and reconciliation – the parables of God's mercy	Sunday 24
Unit VI	The second part of the 'Travel Narrative': the obstacles facing those who follow Jesus	Sundays 25–31
Unit VII	The ministry in Jerusalem	Sundays 32–33
Unit VIII	Christ the King: reconciliation	Sunday 34

SUNDAYS IN ORDINARY TIME

Ordinary Time provides the Church with an opportunity to bring out more clearly the importance of Sunday as the first feast of all, the weekly celebration of the Paschal Mystery.

The Sunday celebration serves as a model for all liturgical celebrations in the parish. The standards and norms we establish in our Sunday worship around music, ministry, participation, welcome and Word, should find echoes in how we go about other liturgies in the life of the community and its members.

When a Solemnity, a Feast of the Lord, or the Commemoration of All the Faithful Departed falls on a Sunday in Ordinary Time, this celebration takes precedence over the Sunday liturgy.

WEEKDAY CELEBRATIONS

Making Full Use of Options Available
Normally a smaller grouping of the faithful gathers for weekday Eucharist than is the case for Sundays. Advantage should be taken of the more intimate setting that this creates, and of the more informal, if always reverent, style of liturgy that can ensue. At all times, however, due respect and care for the liturgy should be a mark of weekday celebrations, just as it is for those of Sunday and other occasions.

Full use should be made of all of the options available in the Roman Missal and the Lectionary. For instance, the various forms of the Penitential Act should be employed as appropriate, along with a judicious use of the various Common Prefaces available for use on weekdays, as well as from others which may be appropriate because of the celebration of a feast or a Votive Mass. As a general rule, the Universal Prayer or Prayer of the Faithful should be included 'in Masses celebrated with the people'.[6]

The basic principle must always apply that choice of readings and prayers is guided by the pastoral needs of the assembly and not the personal taste or outlook of the priest-celebrant. The spiritual good of the assembly remains the primary and principal guide. The priest 'should also remember that choices of this kind are to be made in harmony with those who exercise some part in the celebration, including the faithful in regard to the parts that more directly pertain to them.'[7]

Prayer Texts
On Solemnities, Feasts and Obligatory Memorials, when they fall on weekdays, prayers are chosen which are proper to these celebrations. On other weekdays in Ordinary Time, the priest may freely choose from the prayers of the previous Sunday, or indeed, from any of the prayers given for any of the Sundays in Ordinary Time. Prayers may also be chosen from an optional memorial that may occur that day, or from the Mass of a saint listed in the Martyrology for that day, from Masses for Various Needs and Occasions, from a Votive Mass, or from a Mass for the Dead. The priest may choose the entire formulary or simply the Collect from these Masses.[8]

---

[6] *GIRM* 69.
[7] *GIRM* 352.
[8] *GIRM* 355, 363.

Ministries

Even in the preparation of daily Eucharistic liturgies, opportunities should not be missed to make full use of the variety of ministries: readers, cantors, people to lead the intercessions, Ministers of Holy Communion, and musicians. The slightly more informal context of daily Eucharist should enhance the opportunity to maintain a high standard of liturgical practice.

Music

Music, 'an integral or necessary part' of the liturgy,[9] could be employed, even in a small way, to highlight some parts of the Eucharistic liturgy, making allowance for the abilities of each liturgical assembly: the *Kyrie* chant, the Gospel Acclamation, Eucharistic Prayer acclamations (including *Sanctus* [Holy, Holy], Memorial Acclamation [Mystery of Faith] and Amen), or a sung response to a spoken (or even chanted) Responsorial Psalm, leading over time to the chanting of the Holy, Holy, or the Lamb of God, and other parts of the liturgy. Not everything needs always be sung, but sometimes a few chanted parts would serve to enhance the worship experience without causing undue delay to people attending a weekday celebration of the Eucharist.[10]

Holy Communion

For weekday liturgies, as for Sunday liturgies, full use should be made, where appropriate, of the permission to share Holy Communion from the chalice,[11] as well as to have people (if the number is sufficiently small) to receive from the one bread broken.[12] It is 'most desirable' that everybody receive the Eucharist from breads consecrated at that same Mass.[13]

The Homily on weekdays

A Homily is recommended on weekdays.[14] However brief, the homily should be considered an integral part of the celebration.[15]

Daily liturgies

When scheduling weekday liturgies, parish communities should not forget that the daily worship of the church also comprises the Liturgy of the Hours. The marking of the various hours of the day (principally those of morning and evening) serves to sanctify the day and the whole range of human activity. It recalls the mystery of Christ in and through its offering of praise and thanksgiving. The Liturgy of the Hours belongs to the entire church, and so at least Morning Prayer (and, if possible, also Evening Prayer) should be celebrated in common by parishes. Some parishes gather for Morning Prayer (or Evening Prayer, as appropriate) before the weekday celebration of Eucharist.

> *Prayer after Communion, Second Sunday in Ordinary Time*
> Pour on us, O Lord, the Spirit of your love,
> and in your kindness
> make those you have nourished
> by this one heavenly Bread
> one in mind and heart.
> Through Christ our Lord.
> Amen.

---

[9] *SC* 112.
[10] *GIRM* 39–41.
[11] *GIRM* 283.
[12] *GIRM* 321.
[13] *GIRM* 85.
[14] *GIRM* 66; *LM* 25.
[15] *GIRM* 65.

CHAPTER FOUR

EASTER

This is the day the Lord has made; let us rejoice and be glad.

EASTER TRIDUUM

The highpoint of the Liturgical Year

The Easter Triduum of the passion and resurrection of Christ is the culmination of the entire liturgical year. It is to the year what Sunday is to the week. Through the liturgy of the Triduum, the Church is intimately united with Christ and shares in his passage from death to life.[1] The penitential discipline of the Lenten fast gives way to the Paschal fast and, in turn, moves to feast.

Unity of Celebration and Celebrating Community

The Triduum begins with the Evening Mass of the Lord's Supper, is continued through Good Friday with the celebration of the passion of the Lord and Holy Saturday, reaches its high point in the Easter Vigil and concludes with Evening Prayer on Easter Sunday.[2] We are greeted at the Evening Mass of the Lord's Supper and we are not dismissed again until the closing of the Easter Vigil.

In order to express the unity of the parish community, all religious communities and other groups should take part in the common worship of the Triduum, and where the liturgy of the Triduum cannot be carried out with due solemnity because the number of participants and ministers is very small, such groups of the faithful should, as far as possible, assemble with a larger community.[3]

For the sake of unity, the Evening Mass of the Lord's Supper, the Celebration of the Lord's Passion, and the Easter Vigil are not repeated in a parish, though exceptions may be made, however, in those parishes where it is impossible for all the people to assemble at the same time and place for the Triduum liturgies.

Preparing for the Triduum

The centrality that these liturgies have in the life of the Church calls for their careful and thoughtful preparation, as well as their sensitive celebration. Adequate time and resources need to be allocated to prepare these liturgies and to prepare sufficient numbers of ministers in order that the Triduum celebrations can bear the weight of the profound mysteries that they express and hand on to the Christian faithful.

☞ How is the Easter Triduum experienced as the highpoint of the Church's Year in how we go about these days individually and/or as a parish?

☞ Is there anything in what we have read so far that we need to take on board in our local practice?

---

[1] See *UNLYC* 18.
[2] *UNLYC* 19; see *PS* 27.
[3] See *PS* 43, 94.

HOLY THURSDAY

We should glory in the Cross of our Lord Jesus Christ, in whom is our salvation, life and resurrection, through whom we are saved and delivered. (cf. Galatians 6:14)

This Entrance Antiphon of Holy Thursday's Mass reminds us that we enter these days as believers in the Paschal Mystery. From the opening moments of these days we profess through prayer and deed our faith in the events of the Cross and the resurrection. We are people of faith, celebrating the deepest mysteries of that faith. 'For the resurrection of Christ is the foundation of our faith and hope, and through Baptism and Confirmation we are inserted into the Paschal Mystery of Christ, dying, buried, and raised with him, and with him we shall also reign.'[4]

Eucharist – meal, sacrifice, service, sacrament of unity and love …

The Evening Mass of the Lord's Supper is fittingly the first liturgical action, the opening moment, of the Easter Triduum. It is celebrated in the evening at a time convenient for the full participation of all people.

At the Last Supper, on the night when he was betrayed, our Saviour instituted the Eucharistic sacrifice of his body and blood. He did this in order to perpetuate the sacrifice of the cross throughout the centuries until he should come again and in this way to entrust to his beloved Bride, the Church, a memorial of his death and resurrection: a sacrament of love, a sign of unity, a bond of charity, a paschal banquet 'in which Christ is eaten, the heart is filled with grace, and a pledge of future glory is given to us.'[5]

A homily in action – The Washing of Feet

Christ prayed at the Last Supper that all might be one (cf. John 17:21-23). In a new commandment, he urged his disciples to love one another: there is no greater love, he said, than to lay down one's life for a friend (cf. John 15:12-13). As a sign of this love, Christ, the servant destined to suffer and so to enter into glory, performed an act of love and service in washing the feet of his disciples as recorded in the gospel proclaimed at the Mass of the Lord's Supper. It is followed by the ritual washing of feet in the midst of the assembly, unless there are serious pastoral reasons for omitting it.

The Triduum is not a passion play, recalling historical events; the rite of washing feet is more than a mime in which the washing of feet of several people is enacted. It is a rite in which the presiding priest, assisted by others, performs an act of service, an act which reveals the true nature of Christian love and discipleship and a gospel sign where Jesus showed us what it means to be people of Eucharist. We are called to a new commandment of love and service to one another.

> ☞ In our own families, communities, country … where do we witness people living out this gospel commandment of love and service to one another?
>
> ☞ At our celebration, how might we make this ritual action speak as authentically as possible to people in our community?

Eucharist calls us to charity

Mutual service, typical of Christian love and central to an understanding of Eucharist, is further expressed by bringing to church gifts for the poor. These gifts are some of the fruit of our Lenten

---

[4] *PS* 80.
[5] *SC* 47.

penance. In Ireland, this is when many people choose to return their Trócaire boxes to the parish. There is a place within this liturgy to highlight this practical expression of charity. These gifts can be presented with the gifts of bread and wine.

Gifts of bread and wine

'The tabernacle should be completely empty before the celebration. Hosts for the communion of the faithful should be consecrated during that celebration. A sufficient amount of bread should be consecrated to provide also for Communion the following day.'[6]

This is a night, remembering the command of Christ to *take and eat, take and drink*, to bring forward enough wine to be consecrated so that the invitation to take and eat, take and drink can be extended to the assembly.

'*Ubi caritas et amor, Deus ibi est*' (Where charity or love are found, there is God) or another suitable hymn is suggested at this time. It reminds us once again of the central themes of Eucharist.

Provision should also be made for those who are house-bound or ill to receive Communion.

☛ Discuss the practical implications of above for the preparation of the altar and presentation of the gifts in your parish.

☛ How does your parish respond to the gospel call of mutual service and charity?

Transfer of the Eucharist to a Place of Reservation

The Mass of the Lord's Supper ends with the Prayer after Communion, omitting the blessing and dismissal, and followed by the solemn transfer of the Eucharist to the Blessed Sacrament chapel or a suitable place of reservation where prayer before the Blessed Sacrament may continue until midnight. This period of Eucharistic adoration may be accompanied by the reading of some of the Gospel of Saint John (chapters 13-17).[7]

Stripping of the altar

After the transfer of the Blessed Sacrament is completed, the altar is stripped in readiness for the gathering on Friday, crosses are removed from the church or covered, votive lights are extinguished. If it has not already been done, the baptismal font and holy water fonts are emptied.

GOOD FRIDAY

We glorify your cross and praise your resurrection, for by this holy wood joy came to the world.

On the afternoon of Good Friday, the Christian faithful assemble to recall the death of Jesus 'in sure hope of rising again' (Prayer over the People). It is a *celebration* of the Passion of the Risen Lord because the resurrection is not separated from Jesus' death. 'On this day, in accordance with ancient tradition, the Church does not celebrate the Eucharist.'[8] Also following ancient tradition, the order of the celebration consists of: the Liturgy of the Word, Adoration of the Holy Cross and Holy Communion.

---

[6] *PS* 48.
[7] See *PS* 56.
[8] *PS* 59.

The church has been stripped bare and is at its most sparse, and the gathering on this day, and indeed the leave-taking, is one of prayer-filled silence, with no introduction and greeting or blessing and dismissal.

Liturgy of the Word

Today's liturgy demands and needs our best reading – from the powerful proclamation of Isaiah through to the announcement of the Passion. The first music of the day is the responsorial psalm, already used on Palm Sunday. The proclamation of the Passion is followed by a homily, silence and the Universal Prayers.

Adoration of the Holy Cross

The adoration of the cross focuses not so much on a figure of the crucified as on the cross itself; it is a symbol of victory and salvation. Together with the proclamation of the Passion this is the central action of today's liturgy. To allow for the full symbolism of this rite, only one cross should be used that is of appropriate size and beauty.[9]

Holy Communion

The Blessed Sacrament consecrated and reserved on Holy Thursday is brought from the chapel of reservation to be shared among the faithful. The people pray together the Lord's Prayer and respond to the invitation to the table.

HOLY SATURDAY

> *A day of waiting in expectation and joy.*

On Holy Saturday the Church waits at the tomb of the Lord, meditating on his suffering and death and looking forward to the holy night of the Easter Vigil. The altar is left bare, and the sacrifice of the Mass is not celebrated. On this day Holy Communion is given only as Viaticum (sacrament of the dying).

THE EASTER VIGIL

> *This is the night*
> *When Jesus Christ broke the chains of death*
> *And in triumphant glory rose from the grave.*
>
> *Rejoice, O mother Church, with all your children,*
> *Resplendent in your risen Saviour's light!*
> (taken from the *Easter Exultet*)

The Mother of All Vigils

On this holy night, called the 'mother of all vigils', the Church keeps watch, celebrating the resurrection of Christ in the sacraments and awaiting his return in glory. It is the turning point of the Triduum, the Passover of the new covenant which marks Christ's passage from death to life.[10] It is this Mystery of Faith, the Paschal Mystery, which underpins every Eucharist.

---

[9] *PS* 67, 69.
[10] See *UNLYC* 21.

A Night Vigil

Prefigured in the Hebrew Passover, the Passover of Christ is the night of true liberation in which 'destroying the bonds of death, Christ rose as victor from the depths' (*Exultet*). Therefore, the Easter Vigil takes place at night. It should not begin before nightfall; it should end before daybreak on Sunday.[11]

The Easter Vigil unfolds in four parts:

Service of Light	*- Light*
Liturgy of the Word	*- Word*
Liturgy of Baptism	*- Baptism*
Liturgy of the Eucharist	*- Eucharist.*

Light

The service of light gathers and readies us as one community to hear the Word of God. It begins by the Easter fire. The fire is blessed and the Easter candle is prepared. Reminiscent of the Israelites who were led at night by a pillar of fire, those gathered around the fire are led by the candle into the Church. Then in the light of the Easter candle and the congregation's individual candles, the singing of the *Exultet* concludes this part of the Vigil.

Word

It is the telling of our story that is at the heart of our experience of 'vigiling'. In the light of Easter faith, in the light of the Easter candle, the Christian community waits and listens. In the stories of creation, liberation and rebirth we hear not 'history' but 'our story'.

Nine readings are provided, seven from the Old Testament and two from the New Testament (the Epistle and the Gospel). These nine stories trace the outstanding events of the history of salvation understood in the light of the *Exultet*, the Easter proclamation just heard. At least three readings from the Old Testament should be read. For pastoral reasons the number of Old Testament readings can be reduced to as little as two, with Exodus 14 never being omitted. However, given that the Word of God is at the heart of our act of keeping vigil, we should aim to give people a real experience of waiting and listening.

The faithful reflect on each reading by singing the responsorial psalm, by silence, and by listening and responding to the prayer proclaimed by the priest.

---

[11] *PS 78.*

THE EASTER VIGIL READINGS

I. Genesis 1:1-2:2. *God saw all that he had made, and indeed it was very good.*
The understanding of Baptism as our new creation in the image of God makes this first reading appropriate on this night. This is a proclamation to the catechumens and the already baptised of God's creative work at all times.

II. Genesis 22:1-18. *The sacrifice of Abraham, our father in faith.*
The Isaac story has been seen by Christians from the beginning as a type of Christ's sacrifice. The carrying of the wood represents the cross, and his reprieve from death is seen as a kind of resurrection.

III. Exodus 14:15-15:1. *The Israelites went on dry ground right through the sea.*
This is the most important reading of the night. The crossing of the sea is the type of Christ's death and resurrection, and of the Christian's journey in baptism through dying and rising with Christ.

IV. Isaiah 54:5-14. *With everlasting love I will have compassion on you, says the Lord, your Redeemer.*
This passage in which Deutero-Isaiah speaks of the return from exile has several pictures. In the exodus God had taken Israel as a bride; in the exile he had rejected her, but only for a moment; in his compassion he brings her back. Christ's compassion for his Church is seen in his death and resurrection. The new Jerusalem, the new kingdom is rebuilt with precious stones; the Church shines forth in splendour.

V. Isaiah 55:1-11. *Salvation is freely offered to all.*
The images of Egyptian captivity and Babylonian exile are used tonight to speak to us of alienation from God. We are called to return to him from the land of our enemies, to enter into the full life of the Church.

VII. Ezekiel 36:16-28. *I shall pour clean water over you and you will be cleansed; I shall give you a new heart, and put a new spirit in you.*
Exile was a punishment for Israel's sin; return demands purification, new heart, new spirit. This is achieved for the Christian through Baptism, in which new birth and a new spirit is achieved through Christ's death and resurrection.

VIII. Romans 6:3-11. *New life through Baptism.*
This reading prepares us for the celebration and renewal of baptismal vows. In union with Christ we imitate his death and rising. We go from death to life, from darkness to light, from captivity to freedom, from the old way of life to the new.

IX. Matthew 28:1-10. *He has risen from the dead and now he is going before you into Galilee.*
  Mark 16:1-7. *Jesus of Nazareth, who was crucified, has risen.*
  Luke 24:1-12. *Why look among the dead for someone who is alive?* [12]

☛   What do these Old and New Testament passages tell us about our Christian faith?

---

[12] Taken from commentaries on the readings at the Easter Vigil in the late Brian Magee and others, *In the Light of Christ*, Veritas, 1994.

With the singing of the Gloria we welcome back the church bells that have fallen silent since the Gloria of the Holy Thursday evening liturgy. This hymn points towards the proclamation of the good news about Jesus.

The Collect is prayed:
> O God, who make this most sacred night radiant
> with the glory of the Lord's Resurrection,
> stir up in your Church a spirit of adoption,
> so that, renewed in body and mind,
> we may render you undivided service.
> Through our Lord Jesus Christ, your Son,
> who lives and reigns with you in the unity of the Holy Spirit,
> one God, for ever and ever.
> Amen.

The Easter Alleluia is sung as another proclamation of the Risen Lord. If a Book of the Gospels is used it can be carried aloft through the body of people, with incense and the accompanying use of Psalm 117, with the refrain: Alleluia!

Baptism

In the light of the Easter candle we have shared our story until we have triumphantly and joyfully proclaimed the emptiness of the tomb and the truth of the resurrection. Because we have done this we can now go forward and do what Christ called us to do – to baptise and share in the Eucharist. Baptism recalls and makes present the Paschal Mystery of Jesus' death and resurrection because in Baptism we pass from the death of sin into life (see Romans 6:1-11). Easter, especially the Easter Vigil, is therefore the best time for the celebration of Baptism. Indeed, without the celebration of Baptism at the Vigil, the blessing of water, the renewal of baptismal promises and the sprinkling lose some of their significance.

> ☞ What does the celebration of baptism at this Vigil contribute to the prayer experience of the people?
> ☞ What does it mean for you to stand and renew the promises of your baptism at the Easter Vigil?

Eucharist

It is through the celebration of the Eucharist that the Church continues to celebrate the resurrection of the Lord. Therefore, while the rite remains unchanged in relation to the Sunday celebration, we should avoid the temptation to rush this element of the night. Indeed, the liturgy of the Eucharist is the culmination of the vigil, when the whole church is called to the table that the Lord has prepared for his people through his death and resurrection. It is the high point of the night's liturgy because it is in the fullest sense the Easter sacrament: the commemoration of the sacrifice of the cross, the presence of the risen Christ, the completion of Christian initiation, and the foretaste of the eternal Pasch.[13]

Before being welcomed to the supper of the Lord's body and blood, the newly initiated share for the first time in the faithful's holy sign of peace.

---

[13] See PS 90.

As on Holy Thursday, this is a night to follow the basic principle that the faithful receive the Eucharistic bread and wine consecrated at the same Mass. On this night of all nights we should consider the gospel invitation of Jesus to take and eat, take and drink.

> *Communion Antiphon 1 Cor 5:7-8*
> Christ our Passover has been sacrificed;
> therefore let us keep the feast
> with the unleavened bread of purity and truth, alleluia.

The Easter Vigil concludes: Alleluia, alleluia!

EASTER SUNDAY

> *Christ, my hope, has risen:*
> *he goes before you into Galilee.*
> *That Christ is truly risen from the dead we know.*
> *Victorious king, your mercy show! Amen. Alleluia.*

The Easter joy of the Triduum continues

The joy of the resurrection, proclaimed and celebrated during the Easter Vigil, overflows into the Masses of Easter day. The Easter candle is alight in the sanctuary, our songs this day are full of Alleluias. It is important to sustain the celebration of the resurrection during this festival day, so that its place as the last day of the Triduum is evident.

Renewing our Baptism

While elements proper to the Easter Vigil should not be repeated, it is appropriate for the faithful to renew their baptismal promises at Masses on Easter day. If done, this renewal replaces the profession of faith and is accompanied by the sprinkling of the people with water from the baptismal font. A song with a baptismal character is sung. The Easter Sunday Eucharist is a suitable time to celebrate the baptism of infants.

The Sacred Triduum concludes with Evening Prayer.

SEASON OF EASTER

> *The company of disciples said: It is true – the Lord has risen*

The shape of the 'Great Sunday' of fifty days

- Easter Sunday is both the third day of the Triduum and the first day of the season of Easter.
- The first eight days of the season, the octave of Easter, are celebrated as solemnities of the Lord. The Sundays of Easter take precedence over all other solemnities and feasts.
- In Ireland, Ascension is observed on the Seventh Sunday of Easter.
- The fiftieth and last day is the feast of Pentecost.
- These fifty days are an unbroken celebration of the victory of the risen Lord; they are celebrated as one feast day, sometimes called 'the Great Sunday'.[14]

---

[14] See *UNYLC* 5, 22–25.

The Character of the Easter Season

Throughout this festive season, alleluias are sung and the Easter candle stands in the midst of the assembly. The water of the font remains an important symbol throughout the season – with the sprinkling of water from the font being most suitable in the Opening Rites of the Sundays of Easter. Christ is risen, he reigns glorious with the Father, and is present through the gift of the Spirit. This is the Easter mystery that is celebrated in the fifty-day feast.

The Word of God in the Easter Season

The Acts of the Apostles and the Gospel of John are at the heart of the liturgy of the word throughout the fifty days of Easter. The Gospel of John offers the community of faith an opportunity to deepen its understanding of the central place that Christ's dying and rising, the paschal mystery, occupies in its life. The Acts of the Apostles shows how the Church derives its entire life from this mystery and its ultimate fruit, the gift of the Holy Spirit.[15]

A season of initiation

The whole season is a suitable time for Christian initiation. Special attention may be given to the celebration of infant baptism. In particular, the Easter season is the best time to celebrate the confirmation of children baptised as infants, as well as their first Holy Communion. Parishes might consider this when scheduling the sacraments of initiation for the children of the parish.

Special attention is given to neophytes, that is, those baptised at the Easter Vigil, making the season of Easter a time for all to deepen their understanding of the Paschal Mystery and making it part of their lives.

Pentecost

The sacred period of fifty days concludes with Pentecost Sunday, when the gift of the Spirit to the apostles, the beginnings of the Church, and the start of its mission to all tongues and peoples and nations are commemorated.[16]

> *From the Preface for Pentecost*
> For, bringing your Paschal Mystery to completion,
> you bestowed the Holy Spirit today
> on those you made your adopted children
> by uniting them to your Only Begotten Son.
> This same Spirit, as the Church came to birth,
> opened to all peoples the knowledge of God
> and brought together the many languages of the earth
> in profession of the one faith.
>
> Therefore, overcome with paschal joy,
> every land, every people exults in your praise
> and even the heavenly Powers, with the angelic hosts,
> sing together the unending hymn of your glory,
> as they acclaim:
>
> Holy, Holy, Holy Lord God of hosts …

---

[15] See *LM* 74.
[16] See *UNLYC* 23.

A Pentecost vigil of urgent prayer

It is recommended that the celebration of Pentecost begin with a prolonged celebration of Mass in the form of a vigil. It is possible to combine the celebration of first Vespers (Evening Prayer I) with the celebration of Mass. In order to underscore the mystery of this day, it is also possible to have several readings from Holy Scripture, as proposed in the Lectionary.[17]

The character of this vigil is distinct from the baptismal character of the Easter Vigil and is rather one of urgent prayer. This is after the example of the apostles and disciples, who persevered together in prayer with Mary, the Mother of Jesus, as they awaited the gift of the Holy Spirit in the upper room.

> ☞ Consider how the parish might maintain the Easter character of this season throughout these fifty days.
>
> ☞ What do you think it means, in terms of how we go about our lives, to be an Easter people?

---

[17] See *PS* 114.

CHAPTER FIVE

LENT

Awaiting the sacred paschal feasts (see Preface I of Lent)

The season of Lent is an opportunity for the Church to renew its commitment to Christ and to more fully embrace the demands and joys of Gospel life. It is a time, a 'gracious gift' when local communities engage in a communal forty-day retreat that focuses on baptism, and penance[1] 'awaiting the sacred paschal feasts with the joy of minds made pure' (see Preface I of Lent).

THE ORIGINS OF LENT

'Lent'
The English word 'Lent' is derived from the Anglo-Saxon *Lencten,* meaning 'spring'. The name in other languages, for example the Italian *Quaresima* and French *Carême,* is derived from the Latin *Quadragesima* (and also the Greek *tessarakosté),* a period of forty days. In the Christian tradition, forty days is understood to refer to a time of intense prayer and preparation; it is a reminder of the forty years Israel spent in the wilderness and Christ's forty-day fast in preparation for his ministry.

Historical Origins
The development of Lent as a period of preparation for Easter began with a preparatory fast for the annual celebration of the Easter Vigil which then developed into the 'Great Week'. The length of this period varied in places but by the end of the fourth century there is a forty-day period of final preparation of catechumens, that is, for the men and women who would be baptised during the Easter Vigil.

With the rise in the number of infant baptisms and the beginnings of the separation of the Sacraments of Initiation one from another, the baptismal character of Lent diminished and was replaced with an emphasis on the penitential dimension of the season. Penitents placed ashes on their heads and engaged in public penance in anticipation of being reconciled at the Eucharist at Easter. When public penance disappeared the custom of all the faithful wearing ashes at the beginning of Lent developed. In the sixth century the start of Lent was moved from Sunday to the preceding Wednesday so that there would be exactly forty days of fasting, reckoning Holy Saturday as the final day of Lent but excluding Sundays. During the sixth and seventh centuries a preparatory period of three weeks was added prior to Ash Wednesday, beginning on the third Sunday before Ash Wednesday which was *Septuagesima* or seventieth day before Easter. The last two weeks of Lent became known as Passiontide, as greater emphasis was given to the passion of Christ.

The Second Vatican Council, recognising the paschal character of baptism and drawing from ancient traditions, reinstated the integrity of the Lenten season by articulating the double focus of

---

[1] See *SC* 109.

baptism and penance: these are reflected in the structure of Lent, the suppression of the Pre-Lenten Septuagesima period and Passiontide, the readings during Lent and, with the restoration of the catechumenate or time of formation for adults seeking baptism, Lent as the Period of Purification and Enlightenment.

- Lent is the forty-day period of preparation that precedes Easter.
- Lent begins on Ash Wednesday and ends before the Mass of the Lord's Supper on Holy Thursday evening.
- Lent has six Sundays (Palm Sunday being the sixth Sunday).
- Lent is the Period of Purification and Enlightenment for those who will receive the Sacraments of Initiation (Baptism, Confirmation, Eucharist) at the Easter Vigil.
- The Chrism Mass takes place on Holy Thursday morning.
- Holy Week consists of the final five days of Lent (Palm Sunday to Holy Thursday) and the first days of the Easter Triduum.
- Eastertide is the fifty-day celebration that flows from it.
- The Paschal Cycle consists of Lent, the Easter Triduum and Eastertide, concluding on the feast of Pentecost.

BAPTISM AND PENANCE

Baptismal Character of Lent

The Constitution on the Sacred Liturgy of the Second Vatican Council stated, 'More use is to be made of the baptismal features proper to the Lenten liturgy' and advised that some of these from an earlier era are to be restored.[2] This mandate was realised with the restoration of the catechumenate and the provision of the ritual book to accompany the variety of liturgies involved in this lengthy period of preparation and instruction, the Rite of Christian Initiation of Adults (RCIA). A special feature was the inclusion of the baptismal Gospels used by the Roman church on the Third, Fourth and Fifth Sundays of Cycle A.

The Period of Purification and Enlightenment commences on the First Sunday of Lent with the Rite of Election when the Bishop or his delegate declares in the presence of the community the Church's approval of the candidates, now called the elect.[3] Catechumens are sent from Mass on the First Sunday to the Rite, often celebrated in the cathedral of the diocese. The Period of Purification and Enlightenment begins, coinciding with Lent as a period of intense spiritual preparation.

Strong reminders of the baptismal character of the season are found in the presence of the elect together with their sponsors and godparents at Sunday Mass. The gracious dismissal of the elect from the Eucharistic community after the proclamation of the Word, the care-filled ministrations of sponsors, godparents, catechists, priests and deacons as they show the elect how to practise the Gospel in personal and social life, guide them and bear witness on their behalf before the whole community,[4] are constant reminders to the wider community of the deeper call and commitment of baptism.

---

[2] *SC* 109.
[3] *RCIA* 108.
[4] See *RCIA* 11.

A way of emphasising Lent as a season of preparation for initiation is to refrain from celebrating confirmations or from baptising infants during Lent (unless of course as emergency or pastoral need may require). Instead, parents and godparents of infants to be baptised on Easter Sunday or at the Vigil may be provided with appropriate formation and encouraged to fully participate in the liturgies of Lent.

For the already baptised, Lent is a time to recall their birth by water and the spirit, their incorporation into the death and resurrection of the Lord. Lent prepares the baptised faithful to re-immerse themselves into the Paschal Mystery by renewing the promises of their baptism at Easter. Lent gives us an opportunity in which we can renew our baptism, reawakening its dynamism in our life and allowing ourselves to undergo a change of heart, a conversion.

Penitential Character of Lent

The penitential character of Lent may be seen in the visual and aural environment of Lent and through the individual and communal expression of the traditional Lenten practices.

'During Lent it is forbidden for the altar to be decorated with flowers. Exceptions, however, are Laetare Sunday[5] (Fourth Sunday of Lent), Solemnities and Feasts.'[6] St Patrick's Day (17 March) is one of the solemnities and always occurs during Lent. In order to highlight the penitential character of the season purple vestments are worn during Lent. On Palm Sunday when the Gospel proclaims the Passion of the Lord, the colour red is used.

The principle of simple austerity demands that the music of Lent focuses on the essentials that are needed to sustain the assembly's singing. The music, while reflecting the more sombre mood of the season, need not be gloomy or dull as the repertoire of refrains and songs of Lent are among the richest in the Church's heritage. During this season the *Gloria* is omitted on the Sundays and weekdays of Lent, though included on solemnities. In a spirit of penitence the Church abstains from singing the Alleluia even on Sundays and solemnities, including St Patrick's Day, until Easter; a Gospel Acclamation, without the word 'Alleluia', is sung.

Prayer, fasting, almsgiving and other works of charity are the traditional pillars of Lenten practices. They reflect the tension of genuine baptismal faith which is both personal and communal, is expressed internally and externally, and leads towards a deeper experience of the death and rising of Christ.

In Preface I for Lent, the season is spoken of as God's 'gracious gift each year', the faithful 'more eagerly intent on prayer and on the works of charity, and participating in the mysteries by which they are reborn', 'may be led to the fullness of grace' that God bestows on his sons and daughters. Preface III prays that 'our self-denial should give [God] thanks, humble our sinful pride, contribute to the feeding of the poor.'

AT MASS DURING LENT

Ash Wednesday

On Ash Wednesday ashes are blessed and distributed at Mass, though this may also take place with a Liturgy of the Word, with the readings as at Mass. With the words of the Prophet Joel, the Church is called to fast and return to God who is 'all tenderness and compassion' (First Reading). The Priest places ashes on the head of those present and says:

---

[5] The Entrance Antiphon begins *Laetare*, Rejoice, Jerusalem.
[6] *GIRM* 305.

Repent, and believe the Gospel.

or

Remember that you are dust, and to dust you shall return.

Sunday Eucharist

Particular attention is to be paid to the word of God[7] which provides 'strength for the faith and food for the soul'.[8] The readings for Lent, as throughout the Liturgical Year, are arranged on a three-year cycle. Cycle A may be used every year by parishes, especially in places where the elect are preparing for their Christian Initiation at Easter. In all years, according to the Gospel of the Year, the Gospel reading for the First Sunday of Lent recalls how Christ is led into the wilderness for forty days and is tempted. The Preface of the day speaks of Jesus 'abstaining forty long days from earthly food' and so consecrating 'through his fast the pattern of our Lenten observance'. Similarly the Gospel reading of the Second Sunday reminds us of how Christ is transfigured on the mountain. On the next three Sundays, Cycle A focuses on baptism, Cycles B on the cross and redemption, Cycle C on repentance and penance. On the final Sunday of Lent, Palm Sunday, the account of the Lord's triumphal entry into Jerusalem is read when the palms are blessed. The Gospel of the day, reflecting the fuller title of the Sunday, Palm Sunday of the Passion of the Lord, tells the account of the Lord's passion.

Sunday Gospels of Lent

	A	B	C
First	Matthew 4:1-11 Temptation of Christ	Mark 1:12-15 Temptation of Christ	Luke 4:1-13 Temptation of Christ
Second	Matthew 17:1-9 Transfiguration of Christ	Mark 9:2-10 Transfiguration of Christ	Luke 9:28-36 Transfiguration of Christ
Third	John 4:5-12 The Samaritan woman	John 2:13-25 Destroy this temple and in three days I will raise it up	Luke 13:1-9 Be converted or perish
Fourth	John 9:1-41 The man born blind	John 3:14-21 The Son sent to save the world	Luke 15:1-3, 11-32 The prodigal son
Fifth	John 11:1-45 The raising of Lazarus	John 12:20-33 The grain of wheat that dies bears fruit	John 8:1-11 The woman taken in adultery
Palm	Matthew The Passion of the Lord	Mark The Passion of the Lord	Luke The Passion of the Lord

The first readings relate the main elements of the history of salvation from the beginning until the promise of the New Covenant. The second readings from the writings of the apostles are selected to complement the Gospel and the first reading, drawing on themes appropriate to Lent.

☞ Given the baptismal and penitential character of Lent, discuss what the above readings are saying to us on our Lenten journey.

---

[7] See *SC* 109.

[8] Vatican Council II, Constitution on Divine Revelation, *Dei verbum*, 21.

Scrutinies

The scrutinies are part of the celebration of Mass on the Third, Fourth and Fifth Sundays of Lent when the elect are present. The scrutinies are rites for self-searching and repentance; 'they are meant to uncover, then heal all that is weak, defective, or sinful in the hearts of the elect; to bring out, then strengthen all that is upright, strong, and good ... These rites, therefore, should complete the conversion of the elect and deepen their resolve to hold fast to Christ and to carry out their decision to love God above all'.[9]

The scrutinies take place on the Sundays, using Cycle A, when three great stories from the Gospel of St John, with obvious baptismal themes, are proclaimed. On the Third Sunday, as Jesus kindled in the Samaritan woman 'the fire of divine love' (Preface) so, like the woman, the thirst of the elect is fulfilled. On the Fourth Sunday, like the man born blind they are transformed from darkness through the waters of regeneration to be made God's adopted children (Preface). On the Fifth Sunday, like Lazarus raised from the tomb, again using words from the Preface of the day, we and the elect are led 'by sacred mysteries to new life'. The baptised too, in different ways, experience the living water, the light of Christ and the resurrected life of Christ as they continue the journey in and towards a deeper communion offered to them by God.

The prayers of the Missal underline the baptismal and penitential character of Lent. An addition in the new edition of the Missal, restoring an old tradition of the Roman Church, is the inclusion of a Prayer over the People at the end of Mass for each day of Lent. The Prayer on Palm Sunday reads:

> Look, we pray, O Lord, on this your family,
> for whom our Lord Jesus Christ
> did not hesitate to be delivered into the hands of the wicked
> and submit to the agony of the Cross.
> Who lives and reigns for ever and ever.
> Amen.

Weekday Eucharist

The weekday readings at Mass reinforce the themes of the Sundays. It is strongly recommended that a homily is given at weekday Masses during Lent to enable those gathered 'to hold fast in their lives to what they have grasped by their faith'.[10] Intercessions for the elect and for penitents is especially appropriate in this season and the Eucharistic Prayers for Masses of Reconciliation may be especially suitable.

At Mass on Tuesday of the Fourth Week of Lent, in the Collect we pray:

> May the venerable exercises of holy devotion
> shape the hearts of your faithful, O Lord,
> to welcome worthily the Paschal Mystery
> and proclaim the praises of your salvation.
> Through our Lord Jesus Christ, your Son,
> who lives and reigns with you in the unity of the Holy Spirit,
> one God, for ever and ever.
> Amen.

---

[9] *RCIA* 128.
[10] See *LM* 24.

- How do we express and live the baptismal character of Lent in our parish?
- How can we enhance our expression of the baptismal character of Lent?
- How do we express and live the penitential character of Lent in our parish?
- How can we enhance our expression of the penitential character of Lent?
- How can we encourage and deepen the traditional practices of prayer, fasting, almsgiving and other acts of charity?

Chrism Mass

The Chrism Mass for the blessing of oils and the consecration of chrism is traditionally celebrated on the morning of the last day of Lent, Holy Thursday, but it may also take place on another day towards the end of Lent. The local Church is united on this occasion in its ministry of service to catechumens, the newly baptised and the sick. In particular, the Chrism Mass, which is always concelebrated, is one of the principal expressions of the fullness of the bishop's priesthood. The concelebration with priests from various areas of the diocese signifies their communion with him as his witnesses and co-workers in the ministry of the holy chrism.

Blessings of the oils
According to the long tradition of the Roman rite, the blessing of the oil of the sick takes place before the end of the Eucharistic Prayer, while the blessing of the oil of catechumens and consecrating the chrism take place after the prayer after communion. When pastoral reasons suggest, however, the entire rite of blessing may be celebrated after the liturgy of the word.

Chrism
The consecration of chrism is reserved to the bishop and it is used to anoint and confirm the newly baptised and to anoint the hands of priests and the heads of bishops at their ordination. It is made of either olive oil, or other plant oil, and perfumes or balsam. Chrism is a sign: by baptism Christians are plunged into the Paschal Mystery of Christ; they die with him, are buried with him, rise with him and share in his royal and prophetic priesthood. By confirmation, Christians receive the spiritual anointing of the Spirit who is given to them.

Oil of Catechumens
The oil of catechumens is used at baptism and extends the effect of baptismal exorcism strengthening those to be baptised to renounce sin and the devil.

Oil of the Sick
By the anointing with this oil, the sick receive a remedy for the illness of mind and body, so that they may have the strength to bear the suffering and resist evil and obtain the forgiveness of sins (cf. James 5:13-16).

Reception of the oils in the parish communities
The oils blessed by the bishop can be formally received and welcomed by parish communities in the diocese. This may take place during an appropriate service at the end of Lent, before the Evening Mass of the Lord's Supper or as one of the preparation rites celebrated with the elect on Holy Saturday. Those who were present at the Chrism Mass may carry the oils in the entrance procession, incense may be used and a few words of reception spoken. Containers for the oils and the place in the church where they are to be kept should be worthy.

Priestly service
Unity in the priesthood of Christ is expressed in Eucharistic concelebration with the bishop, in the participation of the priests in the consecration of the chrism and in the renewal of commitment to priestly service.

Priesthood of the Faithful
Laypersons who minister to the sick, to catechumens and to the families of children being baptised or confirmed should be encouraged to take their place around the bishop at the Chrism Mass. They may assist in preparing the oils of the sick and of catechumens and in carrying them to the sanctuary, and should participate in the usual ministries of reading, music and so on. The bishop may wish to invite the people to pray also for those who will benefit from the use of the oils, that is, those to be baptised and confirmed, the sick and all those who minister to them.

The Role of the Bishop
In exercising his office of father and pastor, the bishop is with his people as one who serves. At the Chrism Mass and during the season of Lent there are opportunities for the bishop to gather the flock of God's people for special liturgical celebrations. Following the ancient custom of the Church of Rome, the bishop is strongly encouraged to gather the faithful on Sundays or on other days during Lent, in the principle parish churches or places of pilgrimage in the diocese, to celebrate the liturgy with them. This will also help to make it clear that initiation, reconciliation and healing are essentially ecclesial acts.

CHAPTER SIX

ADVENT–CHRISTMAS–EPIPHANY

Next to the yearly celebrations of the paschal mystery, the Church considers nothing more important than the memorial of Christ's birth and early manifestations.[1]

This second 'pole' of the liturgical year groups together Advent, Christmas and Epiphany. It is not separate from our celebration of the Paschal Mystery at Easter but is its beginning. It is the dawning of our salvation. As the Lord himself said to Pilate at the time of his Passion: 'For this I was born, and for this I came into the world' (John 18:37).

ADVENT

The Season of Advent

Our liturgical year begins with Advent. The Latin word *adventus* was used to describe the annual visit of a god to his people at his temple, the coming of the emperor to the throne or his visit to a city. In the Church, Advent originated as a period of intense spiritual preparation for the feast of the Epiphany, which was important as a date for baptism.

'Advent has a twofold character: as a time to prepare for the solemnity of Christmas when the Son of God's first coming to us is remembered; as a season when that remembrance directs the mind and heart to await Christ's Second Coming at the end of time. For these two reasons, the season of Advent is thus a period for devout and joyful expectation.'[2]

Advent is a time in which we are invited to enter the living memory of Christ's first coming to us in 'the lowliness of human flesh' through which he 'opened for us the way to eternal salvation' (Preface I of Advent). So Advent is not a mere looking back to something past but an invitation for us to patiently enter through faith, hope and love into the process which began when God himself entered our history and made it his own.

This in turn 'directs the mind and heart' to Christ's return as judge as an event of our future. Preparation for the celebration of the birth of Jesus prepares us for our definitive encounter with him, face to face: 'that, when he comes again in glory and majesty and all is at last made manifest, we who watch for that day may inherit the great promise in which now we dare to hope' (Preface I of Advent).

Even though purple vestments are used during Advent, it is not a penitential time like Lent, but rather a season of waiting in blessed hope for the coming of our Saviour, Jesus Christ, a time of 'devout and joyful expectation'. It is a time when we can rediscover Blessed John Henry Newman's definition of a Christian as someone who waits for the Lord. It is a season in which we are reminded that 'love is patient' (1 Corinthians 13:4).

---

[1] *UNLYC* 32.
[2] *UNLYC* 39.

It is counter-cultural to remain patiently waiting in joyful hope when consumerism has been fast-tracking us into Christmas imagery come the end of Halloween, if not earlier. The structure of Advent itself teaches us a contrary lesson.

'Advent begins with First Vespers (Evening Prayer I) of the Sunday that falls on or closest to 30 November and ends before First Vespers (Evening Prayer I) of the Nativity of the Lord.'[3]

Therefore, the liturgy invites us into around three full weeks of focusing on waiting. We wait in the spirit of Isaiah and the prophets, longing for the coming of salvation hidden in God. We wait too for the salvation now taking place in the world hidden in Christ and the future salvation to be revealed at the end of time. Our waiting will only end when we hear the words: 'enter into the joy of your Master' (Matthew 25:21).

It is only in the final week before Christmas, from 17 December onwards, that the readings and prayers of the liturgy are ordered 'in a more direct way to prepare for the Nativity of the Lord'.[4]

The Prayer Texts of Advent
The Collect for Monday Week One of Advent captures the spirit of the first period of the season:

> Keep us alert, we pray, O Lord our God,
> as we await the advent of Christ your Son,
> so that, when he comes and knocks, he may find us watchful in prayer
> and exultant in his praise.
> Who lives and reigns with you in the unity of the Holy Spirit,
> one God, for ever and ever.
> Amen.

A typically Advent Prayer after Communion asks the Lord to 'teach us to judge wisely the things of earth and hold firm to the things of heaven'.

Similarly the Scripture of the first three Sundays of Advent urges us to stay awake for the coming of the Messiah at the end times. We are told to prepare a way for the Lord at the insistence of the striking person of John the Baptist, who goes before Christ without sure or certain knowledge of the One he is serving.

Only after 17 December does the focus shift to how Jesus came to be born as well as enriching the Alleluia (Gospel Acclamation) verses with the ancient 'O' Antiphons. These give us biblical names for the anticipated Saviour: like 'Wisdom of God Most High' and ending with 'Emmanuel'.

> Alleluia, alleluia!
>
> *O Sapientia!*
> Wisdom of the Most High,
> ordering all things with strength and gentleness,
> come and teach us the way of truth.

---

[3] *UNLYC* 40.
[4] *UNLYC* 42.

O Adonai!
Ruler of the House of Israel,
who gave the law to Moses on Sinai,
come and save us with outstretched arm.

O Radix Iesse!
Root of Jesse,
set up a sign to the peoples,
come to save us,
and delay no more.

O Clavis David!
Key of David,
who open the gates of the eternal kingdom,
come to liberate from prison
the captive who lives in darkness.

O Oriens!
Morning star,
radiance of eternal light, sun of justice,
come and enlighten those who live in darkness
and in the shadow of death.

O Rex Gentium!
King of the peoples
and corner-stone of the Church,
come and save us
whom you made from the dust of the earth.

O Emmanuel!
Emmanuel,
our king and lawgiver,
come and save us,
Lord our God.

Alleluia!

Symbols in Advent

The lighting of an Advent wreath is a tradition followed in many Christian homes during this season as well as in our churches. It features a candle for each Sunday of Advent on a circle of evergreens, and the week-by-week increase in light in the dark of winter can help indicate the approaching dawning brightness of God's promised Redeemer. Similarly a Jesse Tree featuring symbols of the Old Testament patriarchs can help unite us to their longing for the day of God's appearing.

It would also be supportive of these messages about Advent given to us by the liturgy not to introduce a crib to our church interiors until after 17 December, nor to take from the Advent wreath by the presence of a Christmas tree with distracting flashing lights.

It is in this final week of Advent that the role of the Blessed Virgin Mary features prominently, that period of Advent in which we can spend 'in the womb of Mary', as the poet Jessica Powers put it, where Mary 'longed for him with love beyond all telling' (Preface II of Advent).

THE NATIVITY OF THE LORD – CHRISTMAS

The Origins of Christmas

There is a hypothesis that in choosing 25 December for the feast of the Nativity of the Lord, the early Roman Church was seeking to oppose the pagan feast of *Natalis Solis Invicti* (the 'Birth of the Invincible Sun'), a festival linked to the winter solstice on the same day and established around the year 275. It is also possible that the Roman state authorities may have been establishing a feast in response to a growing Christian presence.

In Ireland we are very aware, from the pre-Christian focus on the winter solstice at places like Newgrange, that humanity in the Northern hemisphere has had a profound awareness of the importance of this turning point of the solar year. It is the time when the encroaching darkness recedes and the light prevails. The birth of Christ was thus celebrated as the true 'sun of righteousness … with healing in its wings' (cf. Malachi 3:20; Luke 1:78), God turning our darkness into a Holy Night.

There was also an ancient tradition which held that Jesus was conceived on the same day and month on which he died, speculated as 25 March, but this appears to have been an explanation for the date of the celebration of Christmas rather than a source of it.

Documentary evidence shows that the feast of Christmas was celebrated in Rome by 354 at the latest and to some extent, perhaps, as early as 336. Other scholars suggest that the celebration of Christmas had its origins in North Africa. In Bethlehem, the completion of the Basilica of the Nativity as early as 314 indicates a possible strong tradition of liturgical celebration in that place from earlier times.

The new feast spread rapidly throughout the Christian world. Perhaps this was due to its being a liturgical expression of the profession of Christ as true God and true man as defined at the Council of Nicea in 325. This feast remains particularly attractive to many people because in it we encounter our God who makes his home in the world and with-us (*Emmanuel,* God-with-us).

The Structure of Christmas

Christmas has its own Octave and it runs from Evening Prayer I of Christmas until the Sunday after Epiphany or after 6 January, inclusive. The Mass of the vigil of Christmas is used on the evening of 24 December, either before or after Evening Prayer I.

We still have the custom of three Christmas Masses in the Missal: one at Midnight, one at Dawn and one for Christmas day. This reflects how the Pope used to celebrate three stational Masses at Christmas: one in St Mary Major's at midnight, corresponding to the vigil and Mass at Bethlehem, in St Anastasia's at dawn, as the Pope visited the Byzantine community, and in St Peter's Basilica during the day.

Preparing the liturgies of Christmas

The celebrations on Christmas Eve and Christmas Day are some of the most popular and best-attended liturgies of the entire year. They are well worth a great deal of attention and thorough collaborative preparation by all those who have a liturgical ministry in our parish communities to make them as full, noble and beautiful as possible.

The crib or manger scene can be of great assistance to all in recalling the story and the circumstances of the birth of Jesus in history and in rekindling a sense of wonder and simplicity. By its design and location, however, it should not displace or overshadow the signs of the Lord's presence and activity in word and sacrament, in the assembly and in its ministers.

Some of the texts and feasts of Christmas

At the Day Mass, in the Prologue of St John's Gospel (John 1:1-18), a Roman contribution to the liturgy of the feast, we hear:

> In the beginning was the Word
> the Word was with God
> and the Word was God …
> The Word was made flesh,
> he lived among us,
> and we saw his glory.

Glory to God in the highest, the hymn inspired by the song of the angels at the birth of Christ (cf. Luke 2:14), is heard on Christmas night for the first time since the beginning of Advent. On this occasion above all others it should be sung by the whole assembly with joy and festive fervour.

The prayers of the Mass show that Christmas is a feast of our being redeemed, and they even draw us back to the end-time focus so strong in our Advent preparation. As the Collect for the Vigil Mass for Christmas says:

> O God, who gladden us year by year
> as we wait in hope for our redemption,
> grant that, just as we joyfully welcome
> your Only Begotten Son as our Redeemer,
> we may also merit to face him confidently
> when he comes again as our Judge.
> Who lives and reigns with you in the unity of the Holy Spirit,
> one God, for ever and ever.
> Amen.

As if to make sure that we do not get too cosy with the image of the child in the manger, the Nativity of the Lord is followed immediately by the feasts of those who were called in the Middle Ages the *Comites Christi,* the martyr companions of Christ: Stephen, John the Evangelist and the Holy Innocents.

The Sunday within the Octave is the feast of the Holy Family of Jesus, Mary and Joseph.

> O God, who were pleased to give us
> the shining example of the Holy Family,
> graciously grant that we may imitate them
> in practicing the virtues of family life and in the bonds of charity,
> and so, in the joy of your house,

delight one day in eternal rewards.
Through our Lord Jesus Christ, your Son,
who lives and reigns with you in the unity of the Holy Spirit,
one God, for ever and ever.
Amen.

First January, the Octave day of Christmas, is the solemnity of Mary, Mother of God. It also recalls the conferral of the Holy Name of Jesus. There is early evidence of a Marian feast on New Year's Day, and on this solemnity of Mary, the Mother of God, we offer Mass for World Day of Peace. The Entrance Antiphon reads:

> Hail, Holy Mother, who gave birth to the King
> who rules heaven and earth for ever.

The crib or manger scene can be of great assistance to all in recalling the story and the circumstances of the birth of Jesus in history and in rekindling a sense of wonder and simplicity. By its design and location, however, it should not displace or overshadow the signs of the Lord's presence and activity in word and sacrament, in the assembly and in its ministers.

The Word was made flesh, he lived among us and we saw his glory …
☛   As an adult Christian, what does it mean for you that God became incarnate?
☛   At Christmas time, what does it mean for us to welcome the adult Christ into our lives, beyond the child in the manger? What are the implications of this?

THE EPIPHANY OF THE LORD

The word 'epiphany' means 'manifestation' or 'appearing'. This feast originated in the Churches of the East and its focus varied from the birth of Jesus, the adoration of the Magi, the baptism of Jesus, the miracle of Cana and others. Each of these Gospel texts involved a particular manifestation of who Jesus is.

Some homilies on the Epiphany from St Leo the Great show that in Rome, by the middle of the fifth century, the main content of the feast was the adoration of the Magi. Our celebration in the Roman Rite focuses on the revealing of the glory of the Only Begotten Son of the Father and of the universal invitation to find salvation in Christ.

The Collect for the Mass during Epiphany day picks up imagery from the Gospel and prays that, like the Magi, we may ultimately find the radiant glory shining from the face of Christ:

> O God, who on this day
> revealed your Only Begotten Son to the nations
> by the guidance of a star,
> grant in your mercy,
> that we, who know you already by faith,
> may be brought to behold the beauty of your sublime glory.
> Through our Lord Jesus Christ, your Son,
> who lives and reigns with you in the unity of the Holy Spirit,
> one God, for ever and ever.
> Amen.

The Preface tells us how:

> For today you have revealed the mystery
> of our salvation in Christ
> as a light for the nations,
> and, when he appeared in our mortal nature,
> you made us new by the glory of his immortal nature.

The Epiphany also gives us the opportunity of announcing the central point of the whole liturgical year: the date of the forthcoming Paschal Mystery. This is announced either after the homily or after the Prayer after Communion

> Know, dear brethren (brothers and sisters),
> > that, as we have rejoiced at the Nativity of our Lord Jesus Christ,
> > so by leave of God's mercy
> we announce to you
> > also the joy of his Resurrection, who is our Saviour.

> On the … day of February/March
> > will fall Ash Wednesday,
> > and the beginning of the fast of the most sacred Lenten season.
> On the … day of March/April
> > you will celebrate with joy Easter Day,
> > the Paschal feast of our Lord Jesus Christ.
> On the … day of April/May/June
> > will be the Ascension of our Lord Jesus Christ.
> On the … day of May/June,
> > the feast of Pentecost.
> On the … day of June,
> > the feast of the Most Holy Body and Blood of Christ.
> On the … day of November/December,
> > the First Sunday of the Advent of our Lord Jesus Christ,
> > to whom is honour and glory for ever and ever.
> Amen.

The Season of Christmas ends on the Sunday falling after 6 January with the feast of the Baptism of the Lord.

CHAPTER SEVEN

WITH MARY AND THE SAINTS

For the feasts of the saints proclaim the wonderful works of Christ in his servants.[1]

'Within the cycle of a year, the Church unfolds the whole mystery of Christ, from his incarnation and birth until his ascension, the day of Pentecost, and the expectation of blessed hope and of the Lord's return.'[2] In celebrating this annual cycle of Christ's mysteries, the Church honours Mary, the Mother of God, 'the most excellent effect of the redemption' and presents her 'as in a flawless image that which the Church itself desires and hopes wholly to be.'[3]

Also included in the yearly cycle are days devoted to the memory of the martyrs and the other saints. In them the Paschal Mystery has been achieved and the Church 'proposes them to the faithful as examples drawing all to the Father through Christ and pleads through their merits for God's favours.'[4]

From the cult of martyrs to the General Roman Calendar

In the early Church, the martyrs, from the Greek *mártus (*witness), in dying for their faith gave the supreme form of witness to Jesus, who was 'the faithful witness' (Revelation 1:5). The martyr was honoured at his or her place of burial each year on the *dies natalis*, the birthday of their martyrdom. This cult included a *refrigerium* or refreshment meal similar to what a family would have at the tomb of their deceased. The Eucharist was celebrated as early as the third century and in time seems to have replaced the *refrigerium*. The *Martyrdom of St Polycarp*, bishop of Smyrna, from around the year 155 is the oldest document about the community gathering 'to celebrate the birthday of his martyrdom each year'. On his memorial, 23 February, the Church prays:

> God of all creation,
> who were pleased to give the Bishop Saint Polycarp
> a place in the company of the Martyrs,
> grant, through his intercession,
> that, sharing with him in the chalice of Christ,
> we may rise through the Holy Spirit to eternal life.
> Through our Lord Jesus Christ, your Son,
> who lives and reigns with you in the unity of the Holy Spirit,
> one God, for ever and ever.
> Amen.

In the course of the fourth century the persecution of Christians ended and they were now able to worship publicly in freedom. The public veneration of martyrs was extended to confessors, that is,

---

[1] *SC* 111.
[2] *SC* 102.
[3] *SC* 103.
[4] *SC* 104.

those who had suffered torture or imprisonment or exile but had survived. A further expansion took place but still based on the idea of martyrdom, when ascetics, who had 'died to the world', Bishops who had given extraordinary witness and virgins were included in the public veneration of saints. While the veneration was local at first, it too was expanded as *Lives of the Saints* and the earlier *Acts of the Martyrs* made them known. Also, the bringing or translation of the relics of a saint to another church or shrine led to veneration in places other than the original place of burial. Local calendars began to include the saints of other churches, leading to the beginning of the creation of a universal calendar, around the sixth century.

Canonisation or the placing of a saint's name on the list or 'canon' was simply *vox populi*, an acclamation by the people, but later was entrusted to the Bishop. The first papal canonisation was of St Ulric of Augsburg, died 973, canonised 993.

'When the liturgy turns its gaze either to the primitive Church or to the Church of our own days it always finds Mary. In the primitive Church she is seen praying with the apostles; in our own day she is actively present, and the Church desires to live the mystery of Christ with her.'[5]

While there was devotion to Mary, since the cult of saints at this early stage was confined to martyrs, she was not included in the ordinary veneration of saints. The earliest feast was of Mary as *Theotokos*, Mother of God, on 1 January, after its definition at the Council of Ephesus in 431. The oldest feasts come from Jerusalem and are celebrated in the West in the seventh century, including 2 February, Presentation of the Lord (though its title changed to the Purification of the Blessed Virgin), 24 March, the Annunciation of the Lord, 15 August, the Assumption of the Blessed Virgin and 8 September, the Nativity of the Blessed Virgin. Other major feasts of Mary are the Visitation to Elizabeth (31 May) and the Immaculate Conception of the Blessed Virgin (8 December). Mary is also commemorated in a special way even in the seasonal cycle, notably on the Sundays and weekdays before Christmas as well as throughout the season of Christmas. In addition an optional memorial of the Blessed Virgin may be observed on Saturdays in Ordinary Time when there is no obligatory memorial.

'The Virgin Mary has always been proposed to the faithful by the Church as an example to be imitated, not precisely in the type of life she led, and much less for the socio-cultural background in which she lived and which today scarcely exists anywhere. She is held up as an example to the faithful rather for the way in which, in her own particular life, she fully and responsibly accepted the will of God (see Luke 1:38), because she heard the word of God and acted on it, and because charity and a spirit of service were the driving force of her actions. She is worthy of imitation because she was the first and the most perfect of Christ's disciples.'[6]

In the Virgin Mary everything is relative to Christ and dependent upon Him.[7] Mary's relationship to her Son and to the Church is clearly stated in the prayers of the Missal, for example, in the Preface for the feast of the Assumption:

---

[5] *MC* 28–29.
[6] *MC* 35.
[7] *MC* 69.

> For today the Virgin Mother of God
> was assumed into heaven
> as the beginning and image
> of your Church's coming to perfection
> and a sign of sure hope and comfort to your pilgrim people;
> rightly you would not allow her
> to see the corruption of the tomb
> since from her own body she marvellously brought forth
> your incarnate Son, the Author of all life.

If the feasts of the Blessed Virgin on the calendar are few at first and those of the saints also relativity small in number, from the eighth century onwards there would be a great increase. Newer feasts of Mary reflected her holiness rather than her role in the saving work of her Son. The emphasis was on Mary as Our Lady.

There were attempts from time to time to lessen the number of feast days and to give Sunday a more prominent place in the calendar and this had effect in more recent times through the reforms of St Pius X in 1912 and by Pope Pius XII in 1956.

Pope Pius XII in his 1947 encyclical *Mediator Dei*, regarded as the first encyclical devoted to the liturgy, faced with the disharmony between the temporal cycle (Sundays and weekdays) and the sanctoral (cycle of saints' days), wrote of one cycle, that of Christ:

> All the year round the Eucharistic Sacrifice and the recitation of the Divine Office revolve, as it were, about the person of Jesus Christ; the cycle being so contrived as to be wholly dominated by our Saviour in the mysteries of His humiliation, His redemptive work, and His triumph.[8]

At the Second Vatican Council, the cult or veneration of saints was affirmed. The saints are both models and intercessors[9] and the Church 'proposes them to the faithful as examples drawing all to the Father through Christ and pleads their merits for God's favours'.[10] Thus 'the feasts of the saints proclaim the wonderful work of Christ in his servants and display to the faithful fitting examples for their imitation.'[11]

Directed by the Council, the Universal Calendar was revised in 1969.

Lest the feasts of the saints take precedence over the feasts commemorating the very mysteries of salvation, only those saints of universal significance are commemorated by the whole Church and others are left to particular Churches, nations, or religious families.[12] A special place is given in the calendar to the feasts of the apostles, the holy men and women of the New Testament, the martyrs, and the saints of the Church of Rome.

The planning for the celebration of the feasts of the saints must take into account the primacy of the liturgical season and should be based on the spiritual good of the faithful. The readings assigned for each day in the weekday lectionary should not be omitted too frequently or without

---

[8] *Mediator Dei* 151.
[9] See Vatican II, Dogmatic Constitution on the Church, *Lumen gentium* 50.
[10] *SC* 104.
[11] *SC* 111.
[12] See *SC* 111.

sufficient reason, since the Church desires that a richer portion of God's word be provided for the people.[13] Eucharistic Prayer I may be used appropriately on the solemnity, feast, or memorial of those saints who are mentioned in it. The name of the saint of the day or the patron saint of the place may be included at the appropriate place in Eucharistic Prayer III.

Solemnities, Feasts and Memorials

The different types of celebration are distinguished from each other by their importance and are accordingly called solemnities, feasts, or memorials.[14]

- *Solemnities* are the days of greatest importance and begin with Evening Prayer the preceding day. They are provided with an entire proper Mass and sometimes their own vigil Mass. The *Gloria* is appropriate in the opening rite and the Creed is used.
- *Feasts* are celebrated within the limits of a natural day. They also are provided with an entire proper Mass.
- *Memorials* are either obligatory or optional. Obligatory memorials are celebrated as given in the calendar. They usually do not have a complete Mass formulary. In most cases only a Collect is given. The remaining texts may be chosen from the weekday Mass or the appropriate common. For the seasons of Advent, Lent, and Easter, texts are appropriately taken from the weekday Mass of the season.

National Proper for Ireland

The National Proper for Ireland, approved 10 July 2007, is incorporated into the new edition of the Roman Missal in sequence with the Universal Calendar.

The National Calendar, when revised in 1972, had only five observances, including one solemnity (St Patrick) and four feasts (St Brigid, St Columba [Colm Cille], All the Saints of Ireland and St Columban). In 1976, a sixth observance was added with the inclusion of the feast of the newly canonised St Oliver Plunkett. In the work of a revision of the National Proper in the mid-1990s, a fuller calendar was proposed and was approved in 1998. This revised calendar allows the celebration of Irish saints in the National Calendar rather than just as diocesan celebrations. This revision of the Calendar allows for a greater Irish identity to be given to it. The National Calendar has one solemnity (St Patrick), three feasts (St Brigid, St Columba, All the Saints of Ireland) and memorials which commemorate diocesan patrons and others. There are seven obligatory memorials: St Ita, St Kevin, Bl. Irish Martyrs, St Oliver Plunkett, St Ciaran, St Malachy and St Columban. Additions to the calendar include Saints Fursa, Gobnait, David, Aengus, Enda, Davnet, Moninne, Willibrord, Aidan of Lindisfarne and Fergal. More recently the memorial of Our Lady of Knock (17 August) and the optional memorials of Bl. Columba Marmion (3 October) and Bl. John Henry Newman (9 October) were added.

The solemnity of St Patrick has been given a three-year cycle of readings. This solemnity and the three feasts also have a proper preface and solemn blessing. The obligatory memorials are given a Collect, Prayer over the Offerings, Prayer after Communion as well as their own Entrance and Communion Antiphons; optional memorials only have a Collect.

---

[13] *GIRM* 355.
[14] *UNLYC* 10.

The Collect for the memorial of Our Lady of Knock is:

> O God, who give hope to your people in time of distress,
> grant that we who keep the memorial
> of the Blessed Virgin, Our Lady of Knock
> may, through her intercession,
> be steadfast in the faith during our earthly pilgrimage to heaven
> and so come to eternal glory with all the angels and Saints.
> Through our Lord Jesus Christ, your Son,
> who lives and reigns in the unity of the Holy Spirit,
> one God, for ever and ever.
> Amen.

☞ Reflect on the place of Mary and the Saints in your prayer life. How do they serve you as both models of faith and as intercessors?

☞ In the parish, how are Mary and the Saints honoured and remembered over the course of a liturgical year and how does this draw us closer to the person of Christ?

CHAPTER EIGHT

SINGING DURING THE LITURGICAL YEAR

The information below aims to assist Church musicians in the decisions they need to make regarding the choice of music for the Mass during the liturgical year. It is also offered to liturgy groups and all who take part in the worship of the Church.

The Mass is the centre of the whole Christian life and the provision of music for its celebration is of the highest importance. Some liturgical singing is, properly, a normal part of every Mass, though this should be particularly so when it comes to celebrations on Sunday or holy days of obligation. Because music is considered integral to worship it is said to serve a ministerial function.

When preparing which pieces of music to be sung, the following table will indicate what is considered priority over all else.

Music of primary importance	• Sung dialogues between the people and the priest celebrant
	• *Sanctus*
	• Memorial Acclamation (Mystery of Faith)
	• Doxology and Great Amen
	• Gospel Acclamation
Texts which were written to be sung	• *Gloria* (Glory to God in the highest)
	• Responsorial Psalm

A more general consideration of music for the Mass has already been given in *Celebrating the Mystery of Faith*, Chapter 5.

To assist Church musicians and for an understanding of music throughout the Liturgical Year, this chapter will focus on those elements which change from one celebration to the next, as well as pointing out features that are particular to certain seasons or celebrations. Some broad principles informing the choice of music will be followed by a more detailed treatment of the liturgical seasons.

THROUGHOUT THE YEAR: SOME GENERAL CONSIDERATIONS

Some pieces like the *Sanctus* or the *Gloria* do not vary as to their text. From celebration to celebration the only concern will be as to which musical setting to choose. Other musical items like the Entrance Song, the Responsorial Psalm, the verse of the Gospel Acclamation and the Communion Song vary from celebration to celebration. It is with these that this chapter is principally concerned.

Responsorial Psalm

The Psalms, as songs and hymns of Israel and as inspired texts of Scripture, were composed to be sung.

- The Responsorial Psalm which follows the First Reading is an integral part of the Liturgy of the Word.
- The singing of the Responsorial Psalm is a very effective way of helping the assembly to internalise and respond to the Word of God.
- The texts to be sung are specifically set out in the Lectionary.
- The responsibility of the musician remains to find a suitable setting for each Sunday, Solemnity and Feast.
- Some resources are listed at the end of this chapter.

Mention should also be made here of the seasonal Responsorial Psalms provided by the Lectionary.[1] A small collection of Psalms for each liturgical season is given and the Psalms may be used to replace the Psalm of the day. As a smaller repertoire, the collection is particularly useful when a congregation is only beginning to get used to singing the Responsorial Psalm.

A common refrain used in Ordinary Time

© Moira Bergin RSM 2011

O__ sing a new song__ to the Lord, O__ sing a new song__ to the Lord.

Gospel Acclamation

The *Alleluia* or Gospel acclamation prepares for the proclamation of the Gospel.

- The Gospel acclamation expresses the people's greeting of the Lord and their faith in his presence as he addresses them in the Gospel reading.
- It is intended to be sung and should rank high in the list of musical priorities.
- As an acclamation, it is sung by all present. The verse is sung by cantor or choir or even recited.
- There are numerous settings of the Gospel Acclamation. A resource is listed at the end of this chapter.

Entrance and Communion Songs and Chants

Entrance and Communion Antiphons are given in the Missal for each celebration. The Antiphon may be sung, either as written or somewhat adapted. Its text is a source of inspiration and may suggest another sung text which is somewhat similar.

Some of the refrains of the Responsorial Psalms, together with the Psalm verses, can also be used at the beginning of Mass or at Holy Communion. The readings of the day will also indicate possible texts. A look at all these texts may often suggest songs which otherwise would not have been considered.

Finally, in many hymnals there are hymns and songs suggested as Entrance Songs and Communion Songs.

---

[1] See *Lectionary*, Volume I, pp. 949–63.

Communion Antiphon, 30th Sunday in Ordinary Time

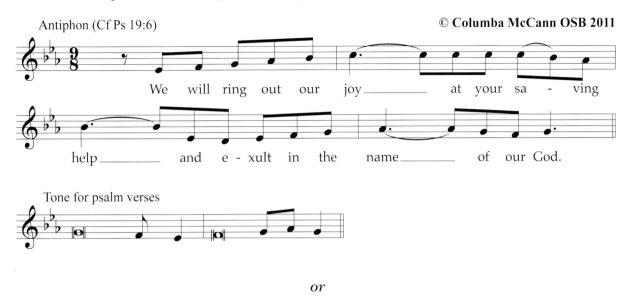

Antiphon (Cf Ps 19:6)   © Columba McCann OSB 2011

We will ring out our joy___ at your sa - ving help___ and e - xult in the name___ of our God.

Tone for psalm verses

or

Antiphon (Eph 5:2)   © Columba McCann OSB 2011

Christ loved us and gave him - self up for us,___ as a fra-grant of - fer - ing to God.

Tone for psalm verses

♪ **Music Planning for each Celebration:**

- Have ready access to the *Missal* and the *Lectionary*
- Check the Readings of the day, Responsorial Psalm and verse of the Gospel Acclamation
- Note the Entrance Antiphon and Communion Antiphon

ADVENT

The season of Advent not only prepares for Christmas but looks forward to the final coming of Christ at the end of time, as well as celebrating the presence of Christ who comes to us in the here-and-now.

Common Responsorial Psalm refrain used in Advent

© Moira Bergin RSM 2008

Here is our God com-ing with pow'r and com-ing to save us.

- *Allow the message of Isaiah and the prophets to guide the choice of hymns:* The Lord gathers the nations in the peace of God's kingdom. The days are coming … The Lord is coming to save us. The Lord is coming to judge. Prepare a way for the Lord. Make his paths straight. Console my people, console them. Exult.
- *Allow the message of St John the Baptist to guide the choice of hymns:* Repent. Prepare a way for the Lord.
- *Allow the message of St Paul and the Gospel to guide the choice of hymns:* We are waiting for the Lord. Live the life that God wants as you wait. Prepare for the Day of Christ. Always be happy in the Lord.
- Stay awake. Watch. Wait.
- With Mary, the maiden with child, know that greater than John the Baptist is among us. The blind see again, the lame walk, lepers are cleansed and the deaf hear, the dead are raised to life, the Good News is proclaimed to the poor.

The 'O' Antiphons

From 17 December onwards the focus is on preparation for Christmas and recalling the events which led up to the birth of Christ. In particular, the texts of the 'O' Antiphons, written originally for use during Vespers, have been incorporated into the verses of the Gospel Acclamations for these days, and enrich the liturgy of the Mass when they are sung. Some musical compositions for Advent use imagery from these antiphons (for example, *O Come Emmanuel*).

In Advent the *Gloria* is omitted, so that its re-appearance at Christmas will be all the more joyful. Notwithstanding divergent practices in the commercial world, it is important to keep Christmas carols for the Christmas season itself, which does not begin until the evening of 24 December.

♪ **Advent**

- The *Gloria* is omitted
- Know the message of our Advent companions, Isaiah, John the Baptist, Mary
- The 'O' Antiphons
- Have Advent carols rather than Christmas carols!

CHRISTMAS

There is a rich treasury of music for Christmas which needs little introduction.
- The singing of the *Gloria*, the song of the angels in St Luke's account of the Nativity of Our Lord, is particularly important at Christmas. It first became part of the Mass of the Roman Rite as a hymn for Christmas.

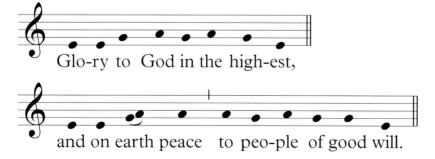

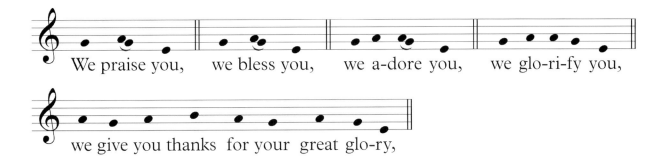

We praise you, we bless you, we a-dore you, we glo-ri-fy you,

we give you thanks for your great glo-ry,

- Christmas carols are an integral part of our keeping Christmas. While most Christmas carols are about the birth of Jesus, the liturgy challenges us to know what this birth means in our lives today.
- The theme of *light* appears regularly, thus suggesting other songs which develop this imagery. This is particularly important on the Solemnity of the Epiphany, in which the story of the Magi is the central focus in our Roman tradition.
- Ordinary Time begins after the feast of the Baptism of the Lord. A rite of blessing and sprinkling of water is especially suitable on this day, and requires music which has a baptismal theme.

♪ **Christmas**

- Sing the song of the angels, 'Glory to God in the highest'
- Christmas is the time for Christmas carols
- 'The Word was made flesh and dwells among us'
- Do something special for the Epiphany and the Baptism of the Lord

---

LENT

Attention to the readings will inspire a much broader range of music than simply picking Lenten hymns from a hymnal. Pay attention to the Sunday Gospels.

First Sunday:	the temptation of Christ
Second Sunday:	the transfiguration
Third, Fourth, Fifth Sundays:	

	Year A:	the Samaritan woman at the well
		the healing of the man born blind
		the raising of Lazarus
	Year B:	the saving effects of the death and resurrection of Christ
	Year C:	repentance and reconciliation.

Lent is about preparing and recalling baptism (see the earlier chapter on Lent). The Apostles' Creed, the baptismal creed of the Roman Rite, is appropriate for the Sundays of Lent.

Lent is a penitential season, and it would be particularly suitable therefore to develop the music of the Penitential Act. The *Gloria* is not sung (except on the solemnities of St Patrick, St Joseph and the Annunciation). The *Alleluia* of the Gospel Acclamation is replaced by another acclamation of praise, and songs which use the word *Alleluia* are either adapted or not used at all.

Ash Wednesday

Ash Wednesday has its own particular requirements, with the blessing and giving of ashes. It is appropriate for the giving of ashes to be accompanied by song. This penitential act follows the homily, and the normal penitential act at the beginning of Mass is accordingly omitted.

Palm Sunday, the beginning of Holy Week

Palm Sunday commemorates both the entry of Christ into Jerusalem, the beginning of the week of his passion, death and resurrection. The readings, prayers and instructions or rubrics given in the Missal guide the selection of music. Care should be taken regarding the choice of music for the blessing of palms and that the music is suitable for singing during a procession.

♪ **Lent: Special Features**

- The *Gloria* is not sung on days of Lent
- *Alleluia* is not sung until the Evening Mass on Holy Thursday and the Easter Vigil
- Do something special for Ash Wednesday
- Music for the blessing and procession of palms on Palm Sunday

---

THE EASTER TRIDUUM

While these notes will consider the days of the Triduum in their chronological order, it is useful to remember that the Easter Vigil is the highlight of the Triduum and deserves priority in planning and resources.

Holy Thursday: Evening Mass of the Lord's Supper

- The *Gloria* is sung at the Mass of the Lord's Supper. This is traditionally accompanied by the ringing of bells.
- It is traditional for the organ to be used only for accompaniment after the *Gloria* of this Mass and up to the *Gloria* of the Easter Vigil.
- The Washing of Feet, recorded in the Gospel reading of the Mass, takes place after the homily. This is accompanied by singing, and the use of a short congregational refrain is very helpful. The Missal gives texts of antiphons which will indicate the general content.

    Antiphon 2   Cf. Jn 13:12, 13, 15
    The Lord Jesus, after eating supper with his disciples,
    washed their feet and said to them:
    Do you know what I, your Lord and Master, have done for you?
    I have given you an example, that you should do likewise.

- It may be helpful to use only short refrains for congregational singing. Thus people can actually watch the rite instead of having to read lengthy texts in leaflets or books.
- *Ubi caritas* is the hymn traditionally associated with the Preparation of Gifts at this Mass.

U - bi ca - ri - tas est ve - ra, __ De - us i - bi est.

- The Mass of the Lord's Supper concludes with a procession during which the Blessed Sacrament is taken to a place where it is solemnly reserved. This procession is accompanied by *Pange lingua* or another Eucharistic hymn. In the case of the former, the last two verses, beginning with the words *Tantum ergo*, are not sung until the procession has arrived at its destination.
- Silence is observed at the end of the liturgy. This silence is maintained at the beginning and end of the next day's liturgy and before the Easter Vigil, giving a sense of continuity between the Mass of the Lord's Supper, the Celebration of the Lord's Passion and the Easter Vigil.

♪ **Mass of the Lord's Supper: Special Features**

- *Gloria*
- Washing of Feet
- *Ubi caritas*
- Procession of the Blessed Sacrament

Good Friday: Celebration of the Lord's Passion

On the afternoon of this day, the Christian faithful gather to recall the death of Jesus 'in their hope of resurrection' (Prayer over the People).

- The liturgy of Good Friday begins and ends in silence.
- There is no penitential rite.
- The Liturgy of the Word requires music for the Responsorial Psalm and the Gospel Acclamation.
- The Prayer of the Faithful takes a different, more ancient form on Good Friday. The congregation answers 'Amen' to each prayer, though a sung response may be used instead.
- The invitation at the Adoration of the Holy Cross 'Behold the Wood of the Cross' and its response are sung three times as the cross is progressively brought into the view of the congregation. A setting is given in the Missal.

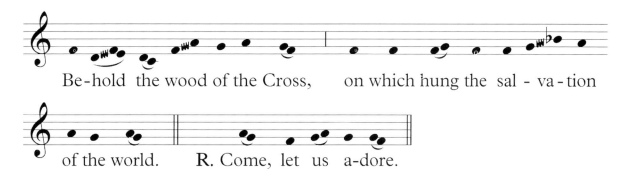

- Additional singing is needed as people come forward individually to venerate the Cross.
- The Communion Rite follows. While this part of the liturgy is similar to the Communion Rite at Mass, it is slightly abridged and no *Agnus Dei* is sung.
- At Holy Communion, appropriate songs are chosen and sung in the usual way.

♪ **Good Friday: Special Features**

- Silent beginning and end
- Responsorial Psalm and Gospel Acclamation
- Music during the Adoration of the Holy Cross
- Music during Holy Communion

The Easter Vigil

The Easter Vigil, celebrating the holy night when the Lord rose from the dead, ranks as the 'mother of all vigils'.

Light

- After the Paschal Candle has been prepared and lit, it is carried in procession through the church, with the acclamation 'The Light of Christ' and response 'Thanks be to God'.

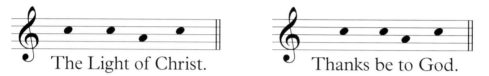

- When the candle has been placed in the sanctuary, the Easter Proclamation, the *Exultet*, is sung by a deacon or by anyone else who has the necessary skill. A setting of the *Exultet* is in the Missal, though other simpler settings are also available.

Word

- Each Old Testament reading is followed by a Psalm. This Responsorial Psalm helps people to enter into this part of the celebration which is at the core of the Vigil and should be given some priority in musical planning.
- After the last reading, together with its Responsorial Psalm and Collect, the *Gloria* is sung.
- The Liturgy of the Word continues with a reading from the New Testament, which is followed by the singing of the Gospel Acclamation.
- This acclamation, the first *Alleluia* sung since the beginning of Lent, takes a particular form:
    - the *Alleluia* refrain is sung three times by the Priest-celebrant (or perhaps by someone else if he is unable to do this);
    - each time it is sung, everyone repeats it; the one intoning it sings it a semitone higher each time; after the third intonation and response the acclamation continues;

\-   instead of having just one verse, this acclamation has a number of psalm verses; it is in fact a Responsorial Psalm with an *Alleluia* refrain.

Baptism

*   When Baptism is celebrated, music includes the Litany of the Saints, an acclamation after the baptismal water is blessed and an acclamation after each person is baptised.
*   When adults are baptised, the Rite of Confirmation follows. Whether there has been a celebration of Baptism or not, a renewal of baptismal promises and sprinkling with water follow.
*   After the renewal of baptismal promises, a song that is baptismal in character is sung during the sprinkling with blessed water.

Eucharist

*   The celebration of the first Eucharist of Easter concludes the Vigil. The music should be especially festive and joyful.
*   The Vigil concludes with the dismissal with *Alleluia.*

Go in peace, al-le-lu-ia,   al-le   -   lu - ia.

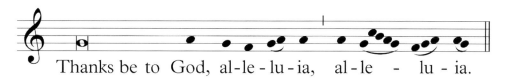

Thanks be to God, al-le-lu-ia,   al-le   -   lu - ia.

♪ **The Easter Vigil: Special Features**

*   'Christ our light. Thanks be to God'
*   Easter Proclamation (*Exultet*)
*   Responsorial Psalms
*   Gloria
*   Special form of the Gospel Acclamation
*   When Baptism is celebrated:
    - Litany of the Saints
    - Acclamation after the blessing of water
    - Acclamation after each person is baptised
*   Music for sprinkling with blessed water
*   Dismissal and response with sung Alleluia

Easter Sunday

*   On Easter Sunday the Sequence is sung before the Gospel. The text for this is given in the Lectionary, and various musical versions are available in a number of hymnals.
*   In place of the Creed there may be a renewal of baptismal promises, which is followed by a sprinkling with blessed water. This sprinkling is accompanied by the singing of a song that is baptismal in character.
*   The Mass concludes with the special dismissal and response sung at the vigil.

♪ **Easter Sunday: Special Features**

- Sequence
- Optional: renewal of baptismal promises and sprinkling
- Special dismissal and response

EASTER SEASON

Easter is a fifty-day feast, ending at Pentecost.

- The Easter Sequence, sung on Easter Sunday, may be sung on each day of the Easter Octave.
- The special dismissal and response are used each day of the Easter Octave and on Pentecost Sunday.
- Pentecost Sunday has its own Sequence which is sung before the Gospel. A text for this is found in the Lectionary, and various musical settings are available in a variety of hymnals.
- The week before Pentecost is a week of prayer for the coming of the Holy Spirit, recalling the waiting in prayer by the disciples with Mary.
- A rite of sprinkling with blessed water at the beginning of Mass is particularly appropriate to this season, and is accompanied by a song that is baptismal in character.
- The Apostles' Creed, the baptismal creed of the Roman Rite, is appropriate during the Easter Season.

♪ **The Easter Season: Special Features**

- Sprinkling with blessed water especially suitable on the Sundays of Easter
- Optional Easter Sequence each day of the Easter Octave
- Special dismissal and response each day of the Easter Octave
- Preparation for Pentecost during the last week of the season
- Pentecost Sunday: Sequence and special dismissal with its response

---

♪ **Some music resources**

Sing the Mass: Anthology of Music for the Irish Church (National Centre for Liturgy)
Responsorial Psalms for Sundays, Solemnities and Feasts (Fintan O'Carroll)
Cantate Years A, B, C (Margaret Daly)
Salm Caintic Cruit I, II (Veronica ní Chinnéide IC)
A Year's Worth of Gospel Acclamations (Cloyne Commission for Liturgical Formation)
Entrance Antiphons for the Church Year (Columba McCann OSB)
The Veritas Hymnal (Jerry Threadgold, ed.)
Feasts & Seasons (John O'Keeffe, ed.)
Hosanna! (Paul Kenny, ed.)
In Caelo (Liam Lawton, ed.)
Alleluia! Amen! (Margaret Daly, ed.)

APPENDIX

UNIVERSAL NORMS
ON THE LITURGICAL YEAR
AND THE CALENDAR

CHAPTER I

THE LITURGICAL YEAR

1.   Holy Church celebrates the saving work of Christ on prescribed days in the course of the year with sacred remembrance. Each week, on the day called the Lord's Day, she commemorates the Resurrection of the Lord, which she also celebrates once a year in the great Paschal Solemnity, together with his blessed Passion. In fact, throughout the course of the year the Church unfolds the entire mystery of Christ and observes the birthdays of the Saints.

During the different periods of the liturgical year, in accord with traditional discipline, the Church completes the education of the faithful by means of both spiritual and bodily devotional practices, instruction, prayer, works of penance and works of mercy.[1]

2.   The principles that follow can and must be applied both to the Roman Rite and all other Rites; however, the practical norms are to be understood as applying solely to the Roman Rite, except in the case of those that by their very nature also affect the other Rites.[2]

TITLE I – THE LITURGICAL DAYS

I. The Liturgical Day in General

3.   Each and every day is sanctified by the liturgical celebrations of the People of God, especially by the Eucharistic Sacrifice and the Divine Office.

The liturgical day runs from midnight to midnight. However, the celebration of Sunday and of Solemnities begins already on the evening of the previous day.

II. Sunday

4.   On the first day of each week, which is known as the Day of the Lord or the Lord's Day, the Church, by an apostolic tradition that draws its origin from the very day of the Resurrection of Christ, celebrates the Paschal Mystery. Hence, Sunday must be considered the primordial feast day.[3]

5.   Because of its special importance, the celebration of Sunday gives way only to Solemnities and Feasts of the Lord; indeed, the Sundays of Advent, Lent, and Easter have precedence over all Feasts of the Lord and over all Solemnities. In fact, Solemnities occurring on these Sundays are transferred to the following Monday unless they occur on Palm Sunday or on Sunday of the Lord's Resurrection.

6.   Sunday excludes in principle the permanent assigning of any other celebration. However:
    a)   the Sunday within the Octave of the Nativity is the Feast of the Holy Family;
    b)   the Sunday following 6 January is the Feast of the Baptism of the Lord;
    c)   the Sunday after Pentecost is the Solemnity of the Most Holy Trinity;
    d)   the Last Sunday in Ordinary Time is the Solemnity of Our Lord Jesus Christ, King of the Universe.

---

[1] Cf. Second Vatican Council, Constitution on the Sacred Liturgy, *Sacrosanctum concilium*, 102–105.
[2] Cf. *ibidem*, 3.
[3] Cf. *ibidem*, 106.

7.   Where the Solemnities of the Epiphany, the Ascension and the Most Holy Body and Blood of Christ are not observed as Holydays of Obligation, they should be assigned to a Sunday as their proper day in this manner:

   a)   the Epiphany is assigned to the Sunday that falls between 2 January and 8 January;

   b)   the Ascension to the Seventh Sunday of Easter;

   c)   the Solemnity of the Most Holy Body and Blood of Christ to the Sunday after Trinity Sunday.

III. Solemnities, Feasts, and Memorials

8.   In the cycle of the year, as she celebrates the mystery of Christ, the Church also venerates with a particular love the Blessed Mother of God, Mary, and proposes to the devotion of the faithful the Memorials of the Martyrs and other Saints.[4]

9.   The Saints who have universal importance are celebrated in an obligatory way throughout the whole Church; other Saints are either inscribed in the calendar, but for optional celebration, or are left to be honoured by a particular Church, or nation, or religious family.[5]

10.   Celebrations, according to the importance assigned to them, are hence distinguished one from another and termed: Solemnity, Feast, Memorial.

11.   Solemnities are counted among the most important days, whose celebration begins with First Vespers (Evening Prayer I) on the preceding day. Some Solemnities are also endowed with their own Vigil Mass, which is to be used on the evening of the preceding day, if an evening Mass is celebrated.

12.   The celebration of the two greatest Solemnities, Easter and the Nativity, is extended over eight days. Each Octave is governed by its own rules.

13.   Feasts are celebrated within the limits of the natural day; accordingly they have no First Vespers (Evening Prayer I), except in the case of Feasts of the Lord that fall on a Sunday in Ordinary Time or in Christmas Time and which replace the Sunday Office.

14.   Memorials are either obligatory or optional; their observance is integrated into the celebration of the occurring weekday in accordance with the norms set forth in the General Instruction of the Roman Missal and of the Liturgy of the Hours.

   Obligatory Memorials which fall on weekdays of Lent may only be celebrated as Optional Memorials.

   If several Optional Memorials are inscribed in the Calendar on the same day, only one may be celebrated, the others being omitted.

15.   On Saturdays in Ordinary Time when no Obligatory Memorial occurs, an Optional Memorial of the Blessed Virgin Mary may be celebrated.

IV. Weekdays

16.   The days of the week that follow Sunday are called weekdays; however, they are celebrated differently according to the importance of each.

   a)   Ash Wednesday and the weekdays of Holy Week, from Monday up to and including Thursday, take precedence over all other celebrations.

   b)   The weekdays of Advent from 17 December up to and including 24 December and all the weekdays of Lent have precedence over Obligatory Memorials.

   c)   Other weekdays give way to all Solemnities and Feasts and are combined with Memorials.

---

[4] Cf. *ibidem*, 103–104.
[5] Cf. *ibidem*, 111.

TITLE II – THE CYCLE OF THE YEAR

17.   Over the course of the year the Church celebrates the whole mystery of Christ, from the Incarnation to Pentecost Day and the days of waiting for the Advent of the Lord.[6]

I. The Paschal Triduum
18.   Since Christ accomplished his work of human redemption and of the perfect glorification of God principally through his Paschal Mystery, in which by dying he has destroyed our death, and by rising restored our life, the sacred Paschal Triduum of the Passion and Resurrection of the Lord shines forth as the high point of the entire liturgical year.[7] Therefore the pre-eminence that Sunday has in the week, the Solemnity of Easter has in the liturgical year.[8]

19.   The Paschal Triduum of the Passion and Resurrection of the Lord begins with the evening Mass of the Lord's Supper, has its centre in the Easter Vigil, and closes with Vespers (Evening Prayer) of the Sunday of the Resurrection.

20.   On Friday of the Passion of the Lord[9] and, if appropriate, also on Holy Saturday until the Easter Vigil,[10] the sacred Paschal Fast is everywhere observed.

21.   The Easter Vigil, in the holy night when the Lord rose again, is considered the 'mother of all holy Vigils',[11] in which the Church, keeping watch, awaits the Resurrection of Christ and celebrates it in the Sacraments. Therefore, the entire celebration of this sacred Vigil must take place at night, so that it both begins after nightfall and ends before the dawn on the Sunday.

II. Easter Time
22.   The fifty days from the Sunday of the Resurrection to Pentecost Sunday are celebrated in joy and exultation as one feast day, indeed as one 'great Sunday'.[12]
      These are the days above all others in which the *Alleluia* is sung.

23.   The Sundays of this time of year are considered to be Sundays of Easter and are called, after Easter Sunday itself, the Second, Third, Fourth, Fifth, Sixth, and Seventh Sundays of Easter. This sacred period of fifty days concludes with Pentecost Sunday.

24.   The first eight days of Easter Time constitute the Octave of Easter and are celebrated as Solemnities of the Lord.

25.   On the fortieth day after Easter the Ascension of the Lord is celebrated, except where, not being observed as a Holyday of Obligation, it has been assigned to the Seventh Sunday of Easter (cf. no. 7).

26.   The weekdays from the Ascension up to and including the Saturday before Pentecost prepare for the coming of the Holy Spirit, the Paraclete.

III. Lent
27.   Lent is ordered to preparing for the celebration of Easter, since the Lenten liturgy prepares for celebration of the Paschal Mystery both catechumens, by the various stages of Christian Initiation, and the faithful, who recall their own Baptism and do penance.[13]

28.   The forty days of Lent run from Ash Wednesday up to but excluding the Mass of the Lord's Supper exclusive.
      From the beginning of Lent until the Paschal Vigil, the *Alleluia* is not said.

29.   On Ash Wednesday, the beginning of Lent, which is observed everywhere as a fast day,[14] ashes are distributed.

30.   The Sundays of this time of year are called the First, Second, Third, Fourth, and Fifth Sundays of Lent. The Sixth Sunday, on which Holy Week begins, is called 'Palm Sunday of the Passion of the Lord'.

---

[6] Cf. *ibidem*, 102.
[7] Cf. *ibidem*, 5.
[8] Cf. *ibidem*, 106.
[9] Cf. Paul VI, Apostolic Constitution, *Paenitemini*, 17 February, 1966 II § 3: *Acta Apostolicae Sedis* 58 (1966), p. 184.
[10] Cf. Second Vatican Council, Constitution on the Sacred Liturgy, *Sacrosanctum concilium*, 110.
[11] St Augustine, *Sermo:* 219: PL 38, 1088.
[12] St Athanasius, *Epistula festalis:* PG 26, 1366.
[13] Cf. Second Vatican Council, Constitution on the Sacred Liturgy, *Sacrosanctum concilium*, 109.
[14] Cf. Paul VI, Apostolic Constitution, *Paenitemini*, 17 February 1966, II § 3: *Acta Apostolicae Sedis* 58 (1966), p. 184.

31.   Holy Week is ordered to the commemoration of Christ's Passion, beginning with his Messianic entrance into Jerusalem.
       On Thursday of Holy Week, in the morning, the Bishop concelebrates Mass with his presbyterate and blesses the holy oils and consecrates the chrism.

IV. Christmas Time
32.   After the annual celebration of the Paschal Mystery, the Church has no more ancient custom than celebrating the memorial of the Nativity of the Lord and of his first manifestations, and this takes place in Christmas Time.

33.   Christmas Time runs from First Vespers (Evening Prayer I) of the Nativity of the Lord up to and including the Sunday after Epiphany or after 6 January.

34.   The Vigil Mass of the Nativity is used on the evening of 24 December, either before or after First Vespers (Evening Prayer I).
       On the day of the Nativity of the Lord, following ancient Roman tradition, Mass may be celebrated three times, that is, in the night, at dawn and during the day.

35.   The Nativity of the Lord has its own Octave, arranged thus:
       a)   Sunday within the Octave or, if there is no Sunday, 30 December, is the Feast of the Holy Family of Jesus, Mary, and Joseph;
       b)   26 December is the Feast of Saint Stephen, the First Martyr;
       c)   27 December is the Feast of Saint John, Apostle and Evangelist;
       d)   28 December is the Feast of the Holy Innocents;
       e)   29, 30, and 31 December are days within the Octave;
       f)   1 January, the Octave Day of the Nativity of the Lord, is the Solemnity of Mary, the Holy Mother of God, and also the commemoration of the conferral of the Most Holy Name of Jesus.

36.   The Sunday falling between 2 January and 5 January is the Second Sunday after the Nativity.

37.   The Epiphany of the Lord is celebrated on 6 January, unless, where it is not observed as a Holyday of Obligation, it has been assigned to the Sunday occurring between 2 and 8 January (cf. no. 7).

38.   The Sunday falling after 6 January is the Feast of the Baptism of the Lord.

V. Advent
39.   Advent has a twofold character, for it is a time of preparation for the Solemnities of Christmas, in which the First Coming of the Son of God to humanity is remembered, and likewise a time when, by remembrance of this, minds and hearts are led to look forward to Christ's Second Coming at the end of time. For these two reasons, Advent is a period of devout and expectant delight.

40.   Advent begins with First Vespers (Evening Prayer I) of the Sunday that falls on or closest to 30 November and it ends before First Vespers (Evening Prayer I) of the Nativity of the Lord.

41.   The Sundays of this time of year are named the First, Second, Third, and Fourth Sundays of Advent.

42.   The weekdays from 17 December up to and including 24 December are ordered in a more direct way to preparing for the Nativity of the Lord.

VI. Ordinary Time
43.   Besides the times of year that have their own distinctive character, there remain in the yearly cycle thirty-three or thirty-four weeks in which no particular aspect of the mystery of Christ is celebrated, but rather the mystery of Christ itself is honoured in its fullness, especially on Sundays. This period is known as Ordinary Time.

44.   Ordinary Time begins on the Monday which follows the Sunday occurring after 6 January and extends up to and including the Tuesday before the beginning of Lent; it begins again on the Monday after Pentecost Sunday and ends before First Vespers (Evening Prayer I) of the First Sunday of Advent.
       During these times of the year there is used the series of formularies given for the Sundays and weekdays of this time both in the Missal and in the Liturgy of the Hours (Vol. III-IV).

VII. Rogation Days and Ember Days

45. On Rogation and Ember Days the Church is accustomed to entreat the Lord for the various needs of humanity, especially for the fruits of the earth and for human labour, and to give thanks to him publicly.

46. In order that the Rogation Days and Ember Days may be adapted to the different regions and different needs of the faithful, the Conferences of Bishops should arrange the time and manner in which they are held.

Consequently, concerning their duration, whether they are to last one or more days, or be repeated in the course of the year, norms are to be established by the competent authority, taking into consideration local needs.

47. The Mass for each day of these celebrations should be chosen from among the Masses for Various Needs, and should be one which is more particularly appropriate to the purpose of the supplications.

CHAPTER II

THE CALENDAR

TITLE I – THE CALENDAR AND CELEBRATIONS TO BE INSCRIBED IN IT

48. The ordering of the celebration of the liturgical year is governed by a calendar, which is either general or particular, depending on whether it has been laid down for the use of the entire Roman Rite, or for the use of a Particular Church or religious family.

49. In the General Calendar is inscribed both the entire cycle of celebrations of the mystery of salvation in the Proper of Time, and that of those Saints who have universal significance and therefore are obligatorily celebrated by everyone, and of other Saints who demonstrate the universality and continuity of sainthood within the People of God.

Particular calendars, on the other hand, contain celebrations of a more proper character, appropriately combined organically with the general cycle.[15] For individual Churches or religious families show special honour to those Saints who are proper to them for some particular reason.

Particular calendars, however, are to be drawn up by the competent authority and approved by the Apostolic See.

50. In drawing up a particular calendar, attention should be paid to the following:
    a) The Proper of Time, that is, the cycle of Times, Solemnities, and Feasts by which the mystery of redemption is unfolded and honoured during the liturgical year, must always be kept intact and enjoy its rightful pre-eminence over particular celebrations.
    b) Proper celebrations must be combined organically with universal celebrations, with attention to the rank and precedence indicated for each in the Table of Liturgical Days. So that particular calendars may not be overburdened, individual Saints should have only one celebration in the course of the liturgical year, although, where pastoral reasons recommend it, there may be another celebration in the form of an Optional Memorial marking the *translatio* or *inventio* of the bodies of Patron Saints or Founders of Churches or of religious families.
    c) Celebrations granted by indult should not duplicate other celebrations already occurring in the cycle of the mystery of salvation, nor should their number be increased out of proportion.

51. Although it is appropriate for each diocese to have its own Calendar and Proper for the Office and Mass, there is nevertheless nothing to prevent entire provinces, regions, nations, or even larger areas, having Calendars and Propers in common, prepared by cooperation among all concerned.

This principle may also be similarly observed in the case of religious calendars for several provinces under the same civil jurisdiction.

52. A particular calendar is prepared by the insertion in the General Calendar of proper Solemnities, Feasts and Memorials, that is:
    a) in a diocesan calendar, besides celebrations of Patrons and of the dedication of the cathedral church, the Saints and Blessed who have special connections with the diocese, e.g., by their birth, residence over a long period, or their death;

---

[15] Cf. Sacred Congregation for Divine Worship, Instruction, *Calendaria particularia*, 24 June 1970: *Acta Apostolicae Sedis* 62 (1970), pp. 651–663.

b)   in a religious calendar, besides celebrations of the Title, the Founder and the Patron, those Saints and Blessed who were members of that religious family or had a special relationship with it;

c)   in calendars for individual churches, besides the proper celebrations of the diocese or religious family, celebrations proper to the church that are listed in the Table of Liturgical Days, and Saints whose body is kept in the church. Members of religious families, too, join the community of the local Church in celebrating the anniversary of the dedication of the cathedral church and the principal Patrons of the place and of the wider region where they live.

53.   When a diocese or religious family has the distinction of having many Saints and Blessed, care must be taken so that the calendar of the entire diocese or entire institute does not become overburdened. Consequently:

a)   A common celebration can, first of all, be held of all the Saints and Blessed of a diocese or religious family, or of some category among them.

b)   Only the Saints and Blessed of particular significance for the entire diocese or the entire religious family should be inscribed in the calendar as an individual celebration.

c)   The other Saints or Blessed should be celebrated only in those places with which they have closer ties or where their bodies are kept.

54.   Proper celebrations should be inscribed in the Calendar as Obligatory or Optional Memorials, unless other provisions have been made for them in the Table of Liturgical Days, or there are special historical or pastoral reasons. There is no reason, however, why some celebrations may not be observed in certain places with greater solemnity than in the rest of the diocese or religious family.

55.   Celebrations inscribed in a particular calendar must be observed by all who are bound to follow that calendar and may only be removed from the calendar or changed in rank with the approval of the Apostolic See.

TITLE II – THE PROPER DAY FOR CELEBRATIONS

56.   The Church's practice has been to celebrate the Saints on their 'birthday', a practice that it is appropriate to follow when proper celebrations are inscribed in particular calendars.

However, even though proper celebrations have special importance for individual particular Churches or individual religious families, it is greatly expedient that there be as much unity as possible in the celebration of Solemnities, Feasts and Obligatory Memorials inscribed in the General Calendar.

Consequently in inscribing proper celebrations in a particular calendar, the following should be observed:

a)   Celebrations that are also listed in the General Calendar are to be inscribed on the same date in a particular calendar, with a change if necessary in the rank of celebration.
The same must be observed with regard to a diocesan or religious calendar for the inscription of celebrations proper to a single church.

b)   Celebrations of Saints not found in the General Calendar should be assigned to their 'birthday'. If this is not known, the celebrations should be assigned to a date proper to the Saint for some other reason, e.g., the date of ordination or of the *inventio* or *translatio* of the Saint's body; otherwise to a day that is free from other celebrations in the particular Calendar.

c)   If, on the other hand, the 'birthday' or other proper day is impeded by another obligatory celebration, even of lower rank, in the General Calendar or in a particular calendar, the celebration should be assigned to the closest date not so impeded.

d)   However, if it is a question of celebrations that for pastoral reasons cannot be transferred to another date, the impeding celebration must itself be transferred.

e)   Other celebrations, termed celebrations by indult, should be inscribed on a date more pastorally appropriate.

f)   In order that the cycle of the liturgical year shine forth in all its clarity, but that the celebration of the Saints not be permanently impeded, dates that usually fall during Lent and the Octave of Easter, as well as the weekdays from 17 December to 31 December, should remain free of any particular celebration, unless it is a question of Obligatory Memorials, of Feasts found in the Table of Liturgical Days under no. 8: a, b, c, d, or of Solemnities that cannot be transferred to another time of the year.

The Solemnity of Saint Joseph, where it is observed as a Holyday of Obligation, should it fall on Palm Sunday of the Lord's Passion, is anticipated on the preceding Saturday, 18 March. Where, on the other hand, it is not observed as a Holyday of Obligation, it may be transferred by the Conference of Bishops to another day outside Lent.

57.   If any Saints or Blessed are inscribed together in the Calendar, they are always celebrated together, whenever their celebrations are of equal rank, even though one or more of them may be more proper. If, however, the celebration of one or more of these Saints or Blessed is of a higher rank, the Office of this or those Saints or Blessed alone is celebrated and the celebration of the others is omitted, unless it is appropriate to assign them to another date in the form of an Obligatory Memorial.

58.   For the pastoral good of the faithful, it is permitted to observe on Sundays in Ordinary Time those celebrations that fall during the week and that are agreeable to the devotion of the faithful, provided the celebrations rank above that Sunday in the Table of Liturgical Days. The Mass of such celebrations may be used at all the celebrations of Mass at which the people are present.

59.   Precedence among liturgical days, as regards their celebration, is governed solely by the following Table.

TABLE OF LITURGICAL DAYS

according to their order of precedence

I

1.   The Paschal Triduum of the Passion and Resurrection of the Lord.

2.   The Nativity of the Lord, the Epiphany, the Ascension, and Pentecost.
      Sundays of Advent, Lent, and Easter.
      Ash Wednesday.
      Weekdays of Holy Week from Monday up to and including Thursday.
      Days within the Octave of Easter.

3.   Solemnities inscribed in the General Calendar, whether of the Lord, of the Blessed Virgin Mary or of Saints.
      The Commemoration of All the Faithful Departed.

4.   Proper Solemnities, namely:
      a)   The Solemnity of the principal Patron of the place, city or state.
      b)   The Solemnity of the dedication and of the anniversary of the dedication of one's own church.
      c)   The Solemnity of the Title of one's own church.
      d)   The Solemnity either of the Title
                  or of the Founder
                  or of the principal Patron of an Order or Congregation.

II

5.   Feasts of the Lord inscribed in the General Calendar.

6.   Sundays of Christmas Time and the Sundays in Ordinary Time.

7.   Feasts of the Blessed Virgin Mary and of the Saints in the General Calendar.

8.   Proper Feasts, namely:
      a)   The Feast of the principal Patron of the diocese.
      b)   The Feast of the anniversary of the dedication of the cathedral church.
      c)   The Feast of the principal Patron of a region or province, or a country, or of a wider territory.
      d)   The Feast of the Title, Founder, or principal Patron of an Order or Congregation and of a religious province, without prejudice to the prescriptions given under no. 4.
      e)   Other Feasts proper to an individual church.
      f)   Other Feasts inscribed in the Calendar of each diocese or Order or Congregation.

9.   Weekdays of Advent from 17 December up to and including 24 December.
      Days within the Octave of Christmas.
      Weekdays of Lent.

10. Obligatory Memorials in the General Calendar.

11. Proper Obligatory Memorials, namely:
    a)   The Memorial of a secondary Patron of the place, diocese, region, or religious province.
    b)   Other Obligatory Memorials inscribed in the Calendar of each diocese, or Order or Congregation.

12. Optional Memorials, which, however, may be celebrated, in the special manner described in the *General Instruction* of the Roman Missal and of the Liturgy of the Hours, even on the days listed in no. 9.
    In the same manner Obligatory Memorials may be celebrated as Optional Memorials if they happen to fall on Lenten weekdays.

13. Weekdays of Advent up to and including 16 December.
    Weekdays of Christmas Time from 2 January until the Saturday after the Epiphany.
    Weekdays of the Easter Time from Monday after the Octave of Easter up to and including the Saturday before Pentecost.
    Weekdays in Ordinary Time.

60. If several celebrations fall on the same day, the one that holds the highest rank according to the Table of Liturgical Days is observed. However, a Solemnity impeded by a liturgical day that takes precedence over it should be transferred to the closest day not listed under nos. 1-8 in the Table of Precedence, provided that what is laid down in no. 5 is observed. As to the Solemnity of the Annunciation of the Lord, whenever it falls on any day of Holy Week, it shall always be transferred to the Monday after the Second Sunday of Easter.

    Other celebrations are omitted in that year.

61. Should, on the other hand, Vespers (Evening Prayer) of the current day's Office and First Vespers (Evening Prayer I) of the following day be assigned for celebration on the same day, then Vespers (Evening Prayer) of the celebration with the higher rank in the Table of Liturgical Days takes precedence; in cases of equal rank, Vespers (Evening Prayer) of the current day takes precedence.